The Four-Hour School Day is for anyone [who] lifelong advantages of home educatio[n] to take the leap of faith into homeschooling and allow Durenda Wilson to be your guide!

KIRK CAMERON, actor and producer

When you're choosing the joy, wonder, and challenge of teaching your kids at home, this is the book you need. Durenda's encouragement and wisdom inspire and will keep you going, even on the rough days.

SARAH MACKENZIE, author of *The Read-Aloud Family* and *Teaching from Rest* and creator of the *Read-Aloud Revival* podcast

Durenda Wilson has written a groundbreaking masterpiece that is sure to revolutionize the way parents approach educating their children. *The Four-Hour School Day* is the most insightful, compelling, and profound book I've ever read on homeschooling.

GINGER HUBBARD, author of *Don't Make Me Count to Three!* and *I Can't Believe You Just Said That!* and cohost of the podcast *Parenting with Ginger Hubbard*

Durenda Wilson's experience in raising and educating her children comes through clearly in this book. It will make you realize you already have what you need to succeed, strengthening your resolve and refreshing your heart. Whether you are a first-time homeschooler or a veteran in need of encouragement, I highly recommend this resource for all homeschool families who want to learn from parents like Durenda who have walked this road with wisdom and courage.

ASHLEY WIGGERS, publisher and co-executive editor, *Homeschooling Today* magazine

In an age of micromanaged childhoods, Durenda Wilson brings calm into the chaos of the homeschool day by encouraging mothers to do less so their kids can learn more. With over three decades of mothering and homeschooling experience, Durenda's wisdom has been hard won, and she's compiled it all here for the next generation. *The Four-Hour School Day* is part memoir and part mantra dedicated to guiding newbies and veterans alike to a simpler way.

JAMIE ERICKSON, author of *Homeschool Bravely* and
cohost of the *Mom to Mom Podcast*

If you want your children to have a strong work ethic and be lifelong learners who are curious and resourceful, know how to handle boredom, pursue their interests, serve others, work together as a family, and independently draw true conclusions, read this book. Durenda describes how and why homeschooling can be and should be more than just a sit-at-the-table-and-read-this-paragraph educational experience. You're schooling for life and not for school. Read this book, and you'll agree!

KATHY KOCH, PhD, founder of Celebrate Kids,
Inc. and author of *8 Great Smarts, Start with the
Heart, Screens and Teens,* and *Five to Thrive.*

The 4 Hour
School Day

Also by Durenda Wilson

The Unhurried Homeschooler

Unhurried Grace for a Mom's Heart

The 4 Hour Hour School Day

How You and Your Kids Can
THRIVE in the Homeschool Life

Durenda Wilson

ZONDERVAN BOOKS

ZONDERVAN BOOKS

The Four-Hour School Day
Copyright © 2021 by Durenda Wilson

Published in Grand Rapids, Michigan, by Zondervan. Zondervan is a registered trademark of The Zondervan Corporation, L.L.C., a wholly owned subsidiary of HarperCollins Christian Publishing, Inc.

Requests for information should be addressed to customercare@harpercollins.com.

Zondervan titles may be purchased in bulk for educational, business, fundraising, or sales promotional use. For information, please email SpecialMarkets@Zondervan.com.

ISBN 978-0-310-36207-4 (audio)

Library of Congress Cataloging-in-Publication Data

Names: Wilson, Durenda, 1967- author.
Title: The four-hour school day : how you and your kids can thrive in the homeschool life / Durenda Wilson.
Description: Grand Rapids : Zondervan, 2021. | Includes bibliographical references. | Summary: "For parents who are concerned about the quality, safety, and care offered in traditional school systems, trusted homeschool expert Durenda Wilson equips you with the resources you need to give your child a great education and a healthy, successful future--and in less time than you think--in The Four-Hour School Day"— Provided by publisher.
Identifiers: LCCN 2021005221 (print) | LCCN 2021005222 (ebook) | ISBN 9780310362050 (trade paperback) | ISBN 9780310362067 (ebook)
Subjects: LCSH: Home schooling. | Home schooling—United States.
Classification: LCC LC40 .W5656 2021 (print) | LCC LC40 (ebook) | DDC 371.04/2—dc23
LC record available at https://lccn.loc.gov/2021005221
LC ebook record available at https://lccn.loc.gov/2021005222

Published in association with William K. Jensen Literary Agency, 119 Bampton Court, Eugene, Oregon 97404.

This book is for informational purposes only. Every state has its own laws, rules, and regulations concerning homeschooling, and the author and publisher make no representation that the suggestions herein will be in compliance in every state.

Cover design: Micah Kandros
Cover illustrations: kalongart official / iStock; Sky Designs / Shutterstock
Interior design: Denise Froehlich

Printed in the United States of America

24 25 26 27 28 LBC 6 5 4 3 2

This book is dedicated to you, courageous parents. The fact that you are considering this book speaks volumes about the kind of parents you are: caring, concerned, and willing to consider taking a leap of faith for the sake of your children. May you find inspiration that will embolden you to embark on the adventure of a lifetime!

Contents

CHAPTER 1

Education

A New Frontier

I had just picked up Luke, our sixteen-year-old, from a drama rehearsal at the local high school. He'd been invited to be part of the technical team and was eager to learn all he could. And it wasn't just this class he was excited about. He was owning every bit of his education and goal setting—and I could *feel* his enthusiasm. He was a bright and social kid, but there was one thing about the other students in the drama class that puzzled him.

"I just don't get why other kids my age aren't excited about all there is to accomplish in high school," Luke said. "They don't seem to care about learning. They don't even want to be in class."

"I'm sure there is more than one reason," I said, "but I think some kids have had so much bookwork piled on them at an early age that they're burned out by the time they get to high school."

It made no sense to Luke because his experience had been so different. His experience as a result of being homeschooled was that learning was an adventure and typically involved more fun than drudgery. Like his siblings', Luke's early school years were filled with lots of playtime. There was bookwork required each day, but for shorter amounts of time than those required of his peers in public school. He had been allowed to follow his interests, which only increased his desire to learn. He had also discovered that the daily reading, writing, and math were simply tools he could use to help him pursue his interests more easily. As Luke's love of learning grew and his body and mind developed, he realized he'd only begun to discover all that there was to learn. It created a fire in him that was largely absent in other kids his age.

Boundless Possibilities

Most kids have a subject or two that aren't their favorite, but the disconnect so many kids experience between their lives and their learning has become increasingly common, not to mention troubling. Is twelve years of drudgery really the best we can hope for when it comes to educating our kids?

I'm guessing this may be a question you've asked yourself. Perhaps you are frustrated and/or disillusioned with your child's current school system. Maybe your child is burned out, discouraged, has little to no interest in learning, or is struggling to learn but doesn't seem to be getting the help he or she needs. You may be concerned for your children's safety and well-being, and you long to protect and care for them but aren't sure how to do that. On the other hand, your kids may not yet even be school age, but you are beginning to be concerned about their educational options, uncertain if the current system will be the best choice. Maybe you picked up this book out of pure curiosity because you can't imagine how kids can get a decent education in just four hours a day. How can that possibly work?

Many parents are beginning to question the status quo, and with good reason. There has been a steady increase in overcrowded classrooms, bullying, teachers feeling pressured to focus on testing instead of nurturing a love of learning, a lack of classroom discipline, a lack of respect for teachers, rising suicide rates among school-age children, and growing drug use among students.

The winds of change are blowing, and the tide is turning when it comes to education. I'm here to tell you there is *hope!* As a home educator of twenty-five years with eight kids, to say I've learned a lot is an understatement. One of the most important things I discovered along the way is that our children can have a rich, full education—an education they love—in a lot less time than we might think. There are many reasons for this, but the main one is that home education allows us to customize our kids' learning to fit their needs, so it's quite simply more efficient.

I know there are a lot of concerns about home education, and I had many of the same concerns myself. Here are the three I hear most often from parents.

- **I don't feel qualified.** Whether parents struggled in school or have a PhD, they *all* tell me they don't feel qualified! But no one knows your kids better or loves them more than you do, and no one is more invested in their lives and futures. It just makes sense that you are the person best equipped to find the resources your kids need in countless areas, including their education. I am a parent just like you. I have no special training, certifications, or degrees, but I know the power of a mother's love. I also know how God has equipped us as moms and dads to be remarkably creative and resourceful, and our fierce love for our kids will motivate us to do what we feel in our hearts is best for them. *This* is what qualifies us to be the best facilitators of our kids' education.

- **My kids might not get a decent education.** There are endless resources available to homeschooling families today. It's one reason more families than ever are choosing to homeschool. But probably the best reason your kids will get a good education is because *you* are helping them get it. The deep love you have for your children and your instincts as a parent are both powerful forces that will help you overcome whatever obstacles you face. If *I* can do this, *you* can do this. So much of education has become a list of hoops for our kids to jump through in order to be deemed "successful." But in an attempt to help our kids by planning every minute of their days, we may unintentionally be sending them the message that they are not capable of being successful without our constant supervision. Homeschooling isn't about creating an environment in which we helicopter parent. It's about creating an environment that allows our kids to grow at their own pace, to become independent thinkers, and to live out their unique purposes unfettered.

- **My kids won't have adequate socialization to become healthy adults.** Outside the traditional school setting, how many times in our lives are we in the same room with people our own age for seven to eight hours a day? Not many. So how does a traditional classroom setting prepare our kids for real-life socializing? Socialization and socializing aren't the same thing. *Socialization* tends to lend itself to conformity.

Socializing is about being able to comfortably talk to people in any and every age group. As the ones facilitating our kids' education, we can make sure they learn the latter.

Homeschoolers have long been stereotyped, but the face of the homeschooling community has changed dramatically in recent years and is continuing to change all the time. In the past, most parents who homeschooled chose to do so for religious reasons, but today, more families than ever are homeschooling for a wide variety of reasons and in many different situations. The number of homeschooling families with a dual income, single parents, an only child, struggling learners, and other unique circumstances is growing exponentially. One must ask why. I believe it's because homeschooling is flexible. Education doesn't have to look like public school—including the long hours—in order to be a rich and full experience. We *can* educate our kids well and in a way that lends itself to our unique circumstances and lifestyle. I can't wait to share more about this as we journey through these pages together.

My Journey to Homeschooling

Because I am an advocate for homeschooling, a lot of parents ask me if I was homeschooled. I was not. I attended public schools almost exclusively, with the exception of a couple short stints in private schools. In fact, because we moved a lot when I was growing up, I attended numerous public schools, about thirteen in all. I don't remember ever having a teacher I really disliked. I do remember classmates who were less than stellar, but my overall experience in public school was very good. For the most part, I felt liked,

I had good friends, and I was reasonably confident in my studies.

It wasn't until late in my teen years that I met a family who homeschooled. Around the same time, I also ran across a book on homeschooling at a yard sale. I'm not sure which came first, but the dots started to connect for me that if I were to have children one day, I wanted to homeschool them. Since there wasn't much information out there at the time, what I did get my hands on was, I believe, a generous gift from God.

Although I had no bad feelings about my own public school experience, I knew I wanted to do something different with my own kids. Part of the reason I think I did so well in school is because I had a secure home life with very involved parents *and* attended schools that were vastly different from schools today. In fact, the school in which I spent most of my time and which had the greatest influence on me was a small country school. Teachers there were given adequate authority and strove for a relationship with students that was built on mutual respect. There was order, peace, laughter, and a sense of right and wrong. Even struggling learners thrived in this environment. Relationships between teachers and students were nurtured. There was a "family" feel in that school. It was a gift for which I am ever grateful. Yet I somehow knew even then that this was not likely to happen for my own children in the public schools of the future.

Several years ago, I was able to thank my favorite teacher from that little country school for his influence on my life. To my surprise, he shook his head, looked me straight in the eye and said, "I had no idea what I was doing. Back in those days, when we were finished with college, there was no teacher training. They threw us into the classroom and simply told us to teach as our favorite teacher had taught us." That was about the best advice this mom had ever heard. I realized at that moment that I had done just that—taken my positive school experiences and implemented them at home with my kids—and it was working!

The Unhurried Path

My kids had some important advantages because they were homeschooled. In addition to eliminating their exposure to a downward spiral in the quality of education, pressure to perform, and negative peer influence happening in the public schools, I was able to apply an unhurried approach. The idea was to slowly ease my kids into a learning environment that involved a structured curriculum. During the first few years of school, we worked for a short time on reading, writing, and math when I thought they were ready. Mostly, I gave them plenty of time and space to play, explore, and experiment. I let most of their schooling be "hands-on," doing things that came naturally, such as taking walks, playing outside, baking, playing with playdough, reading to them, and giving them time to be creative on their own. I also took them along with me to the library, the grocery store, and the post office, talking with them along the way. I wanted their lives to be simple and unhurried.

It seemed unconventional, but something about it also felt right and resonated with my mom heart. My husband, Darryl, and I hadn't necessarily had this type of unhurried school experience ourselves, but we had grown up with a fair amount of playtime and had fond childhood memories. We didn't feel the pressure to perform that so many kids feel today. I think we were given that time because the adults in our lives understood the importance of being able to be a kid. When we began to have our own kids, it seemed as though the demands of school were beginning to choke the life out of children and yielding poor results. We knew in our hearts that having a childhood was an essential part of growing up to be a healthy adult, and it made sense that it would also be foundational to higher learning. We wanted our children to have this gift, and as their parents, we were the best qualified to facilitate that.

Initially, Darryl wasn't 100 percent confident about this unhurried approach, but as the years progressed, he became as convinced as I was. When you have eight kids, you end up with a pretty good experimental test group! The results were undeniable. Our kids were excited about learning because they associated good feelings with the process—feelings of adventure, being able to do exciting and sometimes "dangerous" experiments, and having the freedom to be creative. They had time to follow through on their ideas and see the results, which helped them connect to learning in ways that would not have happened had we made them sit at a table most of the day with their noses in a workbook.

As the years passed, we continued to take this unhurried approach with our younger kids, but we also found that it evolved into a different kind of unhurriedness as our children grew older. I'll share more about this later. More importantly, we were seeing strong evidence that we had made the right decision in home educating our children. By doing what God was compelling us to do, even though it seemed unorthodox, our children were polite, kind, friendly, intelligent, confident, funny, and quickly learning how to think for themselves. They had their own ideas about how to approach life, and while our family is close-knit, many have commented on how very different our children are from one another. They were fiercely independent learners and still are to this day.

The Top 5 Benefits of Homeschooling

Now, mind you, when we first started, I had no idea what the outcome would be. I had to do what every good parent does—learn to listen to the heart God gave me for my children and then follow through, often in spite of what other people thought. It was a walk of faith, but God was gracious to reassure me along the way in ways both large and small. As I look back over twenty-five years on this journey, I can list countless ways my kids have benefitted from a home education. These benefits have changed the course of our kids' lives for the better, and I would do it all over again in a heartbeat. Here are the top five benefits.

Home Education Enables Kids to Learn at Their Own Pace

Having the freedom to learn at their own pace allows kids to find their own way, their own rhythm for learning. This is the brick and mortar that lay the foundation for higher learning. Every one of our kids has had a different time-table for learning. What stands out most to me now is how often it seemed they were *never* going to "get" whatever they were trying to learn, and then, all of a sudden, the dots connected, and not only could they do the work, they *understood* the concepts in greater depth than I thought possible. This didn't happen just once; it happened over and over again. Resisting the urge to compare and allowing my kids the space they needed to learn at their own pace was key to keeping them motivated and becoming lifelong learners.

Each child is unique, and it's a joy to watch their individual talents and gifts slowly emerge as they are allowed to be who they were created to be. Kids in the traditional school setting are under tremendous pressure to perform at standardized levels for their age, and this can be especially damaging in the early years. British teacher, writer, and researcher Ken Robinson put it this way:

> All children start their school careers with sparkling imaginations, fertile minds, and a willingness to take risks with what they think. Most students never get to explore the full range of their abilities and interests. Education is the system that's supposed to develop our natural abilities and enable us to make our way in the world. Instead, it is stifling the individual talents and abilities of too many students and killing their motivation to learn.[1]

Love of learning is snuffed out under pressure. Research tells us that half of our brain function shuts off under stress, and I can only imagine how true that must be for a child whose brain is still developing.

Home Education Allows Freedom for Interest-Led Learning

Over the last two decades, I have watched my kids' interests not only bring life to their learning but also cultivate a strong sense of who they are and what they were made to do. Because they were allowed to explore the full range of their abilities and interests, their school days brought adventure and experiences they wouldn't have had otherwise. Why is this so important? Because kids learn best when they are engaged and interested. Learning is a personal process, and when we homeschool, we have the freedom to personalize our kids' learning so that it feeds their natural curiosity.

Interest-led learning is also important because the career landscape is becoming increasingly specialized. If kids have the freedom to find their niche early on, they can bypass spending the time and money often required to explore options when they are older.

Home Education Gives Kids Strong Roots

When Darryl and I decided to educate our kids at home, one of the main reasons was that *we* wanted to spend time with them. We didn't want our life together to be controlled by a school schedule. We wanted a strong family with healthy relationships because we believed it would help give our kids a solid foundation for future relationships. We wanted to help our kids learn to work through conflict, to see daily how their choices affected those around them, and to become "others-oriented." The roots our children grow during childhood both nourish and anchor them throughout their adult years, so they are not easily uprooted when hardship comes.

Home Education Is Efficient

One of the biggest motivators for our kids throughout their school years was that they could get their bookwork done in a fraction of the time that their traditionally schooled peers could. There was little to no wasted time in our home setting. If they wasted time, our kids were aware it would cut into their free time in the afternoons. They valued that creative space and went to great lengths to protect it, which kept them motivated to get their morning bookwork done. They enjoyed their creative time so much that they didn't realize how much learning was happening then as well. While they were exploring their interests, they were, in fact, preparing for higher education and their futures. When our youngest daughter recently took a class at our local high school, she was amazed at how much classroom time was wasted. In fact, one of the stated requirements for passing the class was simply "putting in your time." How did we move from learning being fun, engaging, and effective to "putting in your time"?

The truth is, we really *don't* have to spend seven to eight hours a day doing school at home because school at home is personalized, which means our kids aren't waiting for other kids in the classroom to catch up, and they aren't being left behind when they're struggling. We can move at a pace that is just right for our kids and ensure that they are getting a solid education and simultaneously becoming lifelong learners.

Many parents are overwhelmed at the thought of spending most of their day homeschooling. One of the reasons I'm writing this book is to show you that your kids actually *can* get their required bookwork done in one to four hours—depending on their age—*and* have an incredibly rich and full education.

Home Education Prepares Kids for Real Life

Because we were intentional about integrating the routines of daily life into their school days, our kids learned what real life requires as we maintained our home, grew a garden, fixed broken cars, grocery shopped, did laundry, planned and prepped meals, helped our neighbors, paid our bills, dealt with conflict, and handled everyday adult life. This enabled our kids to enter into adulthood with their eyes wide open to the duties and tasks that come with being a responsible adult, and each one has entered into that season with a resolve to do it well. That same resolve has overflowed into their work lives as well, earning them reputations for maturity that exceeds their years. This has given them opportunities they wouldn't otherwise have had, and they have thanked us more than once for the critical lessons they learned naturally within the routines of everyday family life.

Even when it comes to "socialization," home education has an advantage because of its close association with real life. Our kids went with us to the post office, library, grocery store, auto mechanic, church, and more. They took some extracurricular classes. We entertained family friends. We went to friends' houses. They were there when the repairman and the mail carrier arrived. They saw what it looked like to interact with all kinds of people every day, so when they entered the work world, they had no problem relating to people of all ages. Home education can, in fact, create adults who are more rather than less socially adept. Because kids haven't been bullied or pushed into social situations but are instead encouraged to overcome obstacles as they are ready, they have the potential to be more accepting and gracious in diverse groups. It's like any other area of parenting or education: thoughtfulness and intentionality are key.

If any of this resonates with you, I challenge you to journey through this book with me, and as you do, to consider home educating for just one year. Think of it as an experiment. I can say with confidence that you won't ruin your kids in one school year. But if you take the leap, I'm convinced you may never go back.

REAL-LIFE APPLICATION

1. What would you say are your biggest concerns when it comes to your child's education?

2. In what ways are you apprehensive about home education?

3. In what ways do you believe homeschooling might benefit your child?

4. Can you see advantages to taking a more unhurried approach?

CHAPTER 2

This Is Us

A Family Snapshot

I sat fidgeting in my chair, unable to focus at my Tuesday morning Bible study. I couldn't stop thinking about our three-year-old daughter. I'd just dropped her off at her first day of preschool, but something didn't feel right.

When I'd decided to enroll her in preschool, the decision had made perfect sense. Instead of just playing in the nursery during Bible study, she would be getting a jump start on her education. She would listen to stories, socialize a bit, maybe learn her ABCs, and participate in educational activities. In the meantime, I could enjoy my Bible study knowing she was being prepared early on for her upcoming school years. It had seemed so perfect, so logical. But now, my heart was telling me something else.

In fact, that something else was all I could think about, and I couldn't help but share it with the older moms at my table. I was in need of prayer, and I told them why. "Oh honey, you'll get used to it. Just give it some time," one mom said. "You've got to let go of her sometime!" said another. I wanted to scream, "But she's only three!" I realized that my second thoughts about preschool were most likely not going to be met with any encouragement in this setting. "Maybe they're right," I told myself, trying to forget about it.

A few more minutes ticked by, but I couldn't forget about it. I excused myself from the group and called Darryl. I told him how I was feeling and asked if he thought I was being ridiculous. As every good husband should, he assured me that I was *not* crazy and told me that if my heart was feeling compelled to pull our daughter out of preschool on her first day, I should do it. In an attempt to be brave and not look like an overprotective mommy, I tried to stay until my Bible study was finished, but I simply couldn't wait any longer. I picked up our second child, who was a baby at the time, headed out the door, and went straight to our daughter's preschool.

As I walked down the hall toward her classroom, I met Darryl, who had decided not to wait until I was out of Bible study to retrieve our daughter. His presence made me feel like we were our own small army about to rescue our daughter—from what, we weren't sure. What we *were* sure of was that this wasn't where she belonged. The class was still in session, so we didn't want to barge in and make it blatantly obvious we didn't want her there. For just a short time, we sat outside the classroom listening, then carefully peeked around the corner unnoticed. Believe it or not, what we overheard in just those few minutes greatly impacted and even confirmed our decision to homeschool our kids.

The teacher was kind but beginning to run out of patience as one child dominated the entire classroom with his lack of cooperation. The other children were trying to follow the teacher's directions, but before they could move on, this little guy needed to be dealt with. Consequently, the well-behaved children were starting to get antsy. It was understandable, as three- and four-year-olds typically haven't yet developed that kind of patience, but the overall picture was somewhat bleak. The potential for learning was completely subject to the antics of the least well-behaved kid in the class, and our daughter was witnessing behavior we had taught her was not OK. Mind you, I am talking about a preschool boy here. My guess is that he would have learned more and been much better off playing outside in the dirt or building blanket forts, so I don't blame him at all for putting up resistance. Neither do I blame the teacher for losing patience as she tried to keep order in the class-room. The simple fact was that this wasn't the best recipe for a healthy learning environment. We wanted more than that for our children. That turned out to be the only day of "school" any of our children saw for a very long time.

We have now graduated seven kids and have just one left at home. I'm no longer at the beginning of our home-schooling journey. The finish line is in sight, and I'm looking back over twenty-five years of home education. It's from this perspective that I want to share my heart and our family's journey in hope that it gives you a fresh vision for your kids' education and future. As our children have left home and started their own lives, I've had many opportunities to see how the choices we made in raising and educating them have positively affected their everyday lives as adults. I'll share a snapshot of where each of our children are right now because I'm guessing it's something you really want to know.

Brittney, our firstborn, is married with three children. My husband and I are extroverts, and Brittney is an intro-vert. At first, I wasn't sure what to do with her. She was shy, and I wondered how much to push her socially. My instincts told me she would eventually grow out of her shyness, and I wasn't going to make a problem out of something that really wasn't one. I regularly engaged her in conversation, encouraged her to talk about her ideas, her interests, her feelings, and what was going on inside, but I tried not to push. We did the things that happened naturally for our family. She attended classes once a week at a homeschool co-op, we went to church, and we got together with friends. I modeled what good conversation looks like, but I never really made it a topic of conversation because I felt it might make her self-conscious.

Brittney made friends along the way. She loved drama class, and one of the reasons she enrolled in it was because she wanted to challenge herself to grow. When she was fifteen, she auditioned for and got the lead role in the spring play. Suddenly, she blossomed and took on a leadership role that defied all evidence she was an introvert at heart. She's never been the same. She continued to grow in confidence and is a strong, gracious soul who isn't afraid to say what she thinks when the situation calls for it.

As a thirty-year-old mom who is homeschooling her kids, she tells me that pushing an introvert is the worst thing a parent can do. She believes she would never have grown so naturally into her own skin if we had not given her permission to do so at her own pace. After high school, she worked as a receptionist at a doctor's office, and the patients there loved her. Not only can Brittney easily talk with people her own age, but with anyone she meets regardless of their age.

Jenna, our second child, is very different from her older sister. From the moment she was born twenty-eight years ago, she let her opinions be known and wasn't afraid to push back. Our children were allowed to have a respectful voice in our home, and Jenna had a lot to say. She challenged me to grow in ways I wouldn't have chosen, and for that, I am eternally grateful. There were some real struggles, but we had the time and space to work on our relationship throughout her teen years. Because we homeschooled, we couldn't isolate ourselves from each other, which forced us to deal with our issues. Consequently, we now have a friendship and a deep and gracious understanding of one another's hearts.

Jenna believes that if she had gone to public school, she would definitely have made some poor choices. When she was in high school, there were times she said she was unhappy about not experiencing "real" school. She later told me that the only reason she occasionally felt that way was because she was being told by her public school friends that she wasn't "normal." This is not something any teen wants to hear, yet she never once asked to actually go to public school. When I asked her why, she told me she had made a list of the pros and cons, and the cons outweighed the pros. Essentially, she analyzed the situation and came to her own conclusion. She was thinking for herself.

Jenna is married with two children and is not afraid to stand firm on many of the current issues facing young moms today. She has an acute gift of discernment that is beyond her years. She is far enough past her school years to look back with a huge amount of gratitude that she didn't give into faulty thinking when it came to "feeling normal." She feels ahead of the curve in being able to discern what's really going on in the world around her and to make solid, adult decisions. Her advice to young people? "The 'cool' kids of today are often the losers of tomorrow." And, yes, she is homeschooling her children.

Jake is our oldest son. He is twenty-six. He was one of

the kids I schooled the least in terms of bookwork. He was always interested in learning how things work, so we initially thought he might have a career in mechanics. Then the internet age dawned, and at twelve years old, he knew he wanted to be a software engineer. He started college at sixteen and graduated at twenty-one with a 3.8 GPA. He earned a bachelor's degree in computer science, with a minor in game programming and another minor in communications systems. He was gainfully employed right out of college.

Had Jake been stuck in a classroom with his day completely planned out by someone else, I doubt he would have discovered what he was made to do at age twelve. In fact, he will tell you that the greatest gift we gave him was the time and space to experiment and follow his interests. What he was essentially doing with that time was *learning how to learn*. More specifically, he was learning how *he* learned. I'm not going to lie; I was tempted to push him at times in certain areas. I'll share more about that later, but there was something inside me that couldn't bring myself to push him because I didn't want to disrupt the good that was already happening. Sometimes, growing lifelong learners simply means getting out of their way.

How did Jake adapt to college? He was involved enough to have fun but never swept up in the kind of college life that might have steered him away from his roots and his own sense of self.

Ben is our second son. I think he started life twenty-three years ago with a smile on his face. Although he didn't read well until he was nine years old, without pressure to perform, he eventually made the connection. Because he was a late reader, early education supporters would have said that he would likely not ever be a good reader or enjoy reading. But he has turned out to be our most avid reader and is passionate about history.

Ben had no interest in college, and we never pressured him to go. We want our kids to own their lives and decisions, and we trust God's unique process for each one. He currently works at a year-round Bible camp and serves as a volunteer firefighter. He's learning all kinds of new construction skills from how to install tile to basic plumbing, framing, and countless others. He loves what he's doing, which isn't surprising. Because Ben was given time to pursue his interests while going to school, he knows what suits him best and doesn't try to fit into a mold for which he wasn't made.

Luke is our third son. He is twenty-two. He excelled at schoolwork but also valued the time each school day when he could pursue his interests. One of those interests was creating digital music. At the time, I wasn't sure how productive that hobby was, but he enjoyed it and was engaged. Eventually, I discovered he had been developing numerous skills that would serve him well a little farther down the road. He tried college, and I'm convinced he would have done well if he had stayed with it, but he chose another path. We have always told our kids that college is just one of many options, and we let our kids make the choice for themselves. The bottom line is that Luke didn't see or experience a lot of real learning in college. To him, it seemed fruitless, expensive, and time-consuming, and, in his estimation, the benefits did not outweigh the costs.

He took a six-month online course that helped him create a career portfolio in audio engineering and operations. He was then mentored by a successful local business owner who took an interest in developing his aptitudes. Luke spent two years using his skills and initiative to bring value to this company, and in return, his mentor shared his knowledge and experience with Luke. Because he is used to thinking outside the box, he was open to learning through apprenticeship.

All along, Luke has had a consistent interest in technology and has been developing skills on his own, such as editing podcasts (including mine). He is now moving forward into a full-time career in audio engineering and as executive director of our family's growing ministry.

By the time our fourth son, twenty-year-old Sam, came along, I was pretty sure I was destined to have boys for the remainder of my childbearing years. It's no small thing for a little guy to arrive on the heels of three older brothers, and Sam's negotiating skills were sharpened at an early age. I often wondered if he would be an attorney because he seemed to think everything was negotiable. As it turned out, he seems able to do just about anything he decides he wants to do. This could have grown from his insatiable desire to keep up with his older brothers.

When Sam was fifteen, he told us he wanted to play on the football team at the local public high school. As his parents, we had to determine if this was a good fit for him. We felt peace about it. We knew it would have its challenges, but we were confident it would be a great growing experience for him. This is the beauty of homeschooling. We know our kids better than anyone. We love them more than anyone, and we get to help decide when they are ready for experiences.

When Sam first showed up for football practice, he was met with a fair amount of teasing and blatant rudeness by several of the team members. He was new *and* he was homeschooled. It was sometimes hard to listen to his stories about how things were going, but I paid more attention to where his heart was, and I could see he was determined to continue to be himself and wouldn't compromise on showing kindness and common courtesy to his teammates.

He went to football camp and, along with learning more about football, he had more than one opportunity to say no to marijuana, even though most of his teammates were using it. This wasn't just about playing football; this was about Sam being able to stand on his own two feet in a setting where the cards were stacked against him. He could continue to stand strong, or he could fall. Either way, he would grow, and that would play a big part in preparing him for life. By the time the season was over, his teammates respected him and considered him a friend.

Not long after Sam graduated from high school, he told us he wanted to work with his hands. He has been gainfully employed for almost two years now, apprenticing as a commercial plumber. There is an increasing awareness that the long-time emphasis on having a college degree is creating a huge need for tradesmen in the market. I truly believe Sam is headed in the right direction. The important thing is that *he* made his decision. He is owning his life.

I thought I might never have another girl, but then Johanna (Jojo) arrived. She is nineteen now. Strong, independent, and empathic, she is blossoming into a beautiful young woman. Just like her brothers and sisters, the free time she's been given during her school days has allowed her to discover what she is passionate about, develop her creativity, recognize the areas she needs to work on, and discover how she learns best.

We spent a fair amount of time during Jojo's teen years having long talks about her faith, the culture, biblical truths, and where she thinks God may be leading her. These aren't conversations that would happen if our daily schedule was packed with copious amounts of book learning and activities. Those certainly have their place, but in a world that seems to be increasingly unstable, helping our kids learn how to be grounded—in their faith and in who they are—is no longer a luxury. It's a necessity.

Our family was at last complete when Silas arrived. His birth sixteen years ago was like being hit by a fast-moving freight train. He was born with transposition of the great arteries and with two holes in his heart. We had no clue until he had breathing problems after he was born. He had open-heart surgery at three days old, and spent the first two months of his life in the pediatric intensive care unit. This meant he didn't get the typical newborn snuggles, nursing, and bonding that is so crucial for development in those first several weeks of a baby's life. Because of that, some of the connections in his brain that help with learning simply didn't connect. That didn't mean Silas couldn't learn; it just meant he would be a different learner and would require more time. Fortunately, since we are a home educating family, I could give him what he needed. I'm finding that if I am patient and allow him to develop at his own pace, eventually he gets the concepts he needs to learn, but it needs to be in his own timing.

I've had Silas evaluated more than once just to be sure we are on the right track. When he was five, a speech and auditory specialist told me that although he would need a little bit of help that they could provide, he was essentially doing really well. She went on to say that if I had sent him to traditional school, he wouldn't be doing nearly as well. This has happened more than once. In fact, one of the teachers who evaluated him wanted to know what I was doing because it was working so well. The funny thing is, I wasn't doing anything particularly "special" or complicated with him. I was simply giving him time, space, love, and encouragement along with a simple, dependable routine at home. He felt secure, and that security has allowed him and our other kids to develop in a way that has stayed true to how they were created.

Silas is now in his teen years and still doing things on his own timetable, but he's certainly not stuck, and he continues to progress. We've noticed that allowing him to be creative with his hands for large parts of each day helps him do better with his schoolwork. That discovery and the freedom to adjust our kids' learning is just another one of the countless ways they have benefitted from a home education.

The twenty-five-plus years of experience and hindsight I'm sharing with you is what convinces me now more than ever that a four-hour school day is not only possible but may very well be optimal. Stick with me through the pages of this book. I plan to take you on a journey I believe will help you gain a much broader vision for your kids' education and set you free to experience the adventure of a lifetime with your kids.

REAL-LIFE APPLICATION

1. Can you begin to envision a bigger picture when it comes to education?

2. Are you recognizing any specific direction for your own child?

CHAPTER 3

The Sacred Cow

"What about socialization?"

This is the question I've been asked most throughout our years of homeschooling. And yet, if a good education is the main reason for sending kids to school, I have often wondered why the first question everyone asks is inevitably about socialization.

Don't get me wrong—it's good to ask questions. In fact, if you really want the right answers to anything, you have to ask the right questions. So let me ask you this: Have you ever questioned the traditional school system's approach to socialization or its outcome? It seems only fair that if we are going to weigh our educational options equally, we should be asking the same questions of each option.

Because my experience as a student in public school was very good overall, it would have been easy for me to conclude what I've heard many parents say: "I went to public school, and I turned out fine." There was nothing in my experience that should have caused me to question public school methodology or wonder if there was a better way. But that isn't what happened.

As I mentioned, I was introduced to homeschooling through a book I picked up at a yard sale and a family I met who were the only homeschoolers I knew. A seed was planted, and I found myself asking more questions and envisioning what life with my future kids might look like if we homeschooled.

Be a Parent First

As our family began this journey and I was faced with deciding whether or not certain ways of learning were a good fit for my kids, my list of questions continued to grow. Or, more specifically, my questions grew when what I was trying to implement as part of our homeschooling day was clearly *not* working. I had questions because I loved my kids. When they struggled, it tugged at my heartstrings and made me question educational issues I might not otherwise have questioned. I *knew* my kids were smart and capable, and I believed they would eventually embrace all they needed to know in order to succeed in life. I couldn't help but wonder if maybe they knew better than I what exactly that needed to be.

Other questions arose when I felt burdened by learning standards set by an unknown somebody somewhere who didn't know my kids. The only way to free myself was to ask good questions that would help me determine whether or not those burdens were really necessary. More often than not, they weren't.

I always tell parents to be a mom or dad first and a teacher second. If we homeschool out of love for our children and the desire to nurture them, teaching and learning will inevitably happen, whether we teach our kids ourselves, find another way for them to learn, or discover they've managed to learn on their own when we weren't looking.

What I've learned along the way is that education is far less about adhering to a narrow system of teaching and more about freedom in learning. When you really think about it, forced learning isn't real learning anyway.

Questioning the Sacred Cow

As I've found answers to my questions and experienced the freedom of home education, I've become even more passionate about encouraging others to embark on this journey. Still, one of the biggest obstacles I've encountered during that process is an unwillingness to question the current educational system. It's often something of a "sacred cow."

The term "sacred cow" is used to describe anything that is considered above criticism; someone or something that is so highly respected it may even be considered wrong to question it.[1] When it comes to education, it seems reasonable to assume that professionals must know more than we do, right? Therefore, we should take what they say at face value and not ask too many questions, even if our instincts are telling us otherwise.

Let me pause briefly to clarify that when I speak of questioning the current educational system, I am not singling out teachers. In fact, I believe there are countless teachers out there who are incredibly knowledgeable, gifted, and have been a blessing to many families. I have had the privilege of being taught by many of them myself. But the educational system within which teachers have to work raises questions that are worth considering.

For example, if we consider the logistics of a traditional

classroom, how much learning time actually happens in a room of twenty-five to thirty kids on any given day? I can imagine that only a fraction of the time might be spent learning and a much larger portion of the time dealing with crowd control and interruptions. I saw this clearly when I was in school myself, and then again in our daughter's preschool setting. According to every teacher I've talked to along the way since then, the ratio of learning time to non-learning time has only worsened with overcrowded classrooms, unruly students, constant interruptions for a plethora of reasons, and a crazy amount of pressure to teach to standardized tests.

In fact, teachers themselves admit that the stress and pressure of teaching have negatively impacted their mental health. A recent survey by the American Federation of Teachers showed that 58 percent of teachers described their mental health as "not good."[2] I have no doubt that many of them are passionate about teaching, truly love their students, and love teaching under normal circumstances—but conditions in too many schools are no longer normal circumstances. Behavioral issues, classroom disruptions, and pressure to raise test scores have tied the hands of teachers. They are stuck within a system that often doesn't even allow them to do what they believe is best for their students.

I've been watching this system now for almost three decades, and I've seen a very clear pattern: new policies are implemented with promises that our kids will turn out smarter and be more prepared for higher education and success as adults, but the results are not impressive.

The NCLB (No Child Left Behind) Act of 2001 was created to promote higher levels of performance by tying federal funds directly to student achievement as measured by standardized test scores. This has proven to be a bad idea for many reasons. Most schools buckled under the pressure and were worse off than before NCLB. Only schools that were already well-funded and not overcrowded showed some improvement.[3] In 2015, the NCLB Act was replaced by ESSA (Every Student Succeeds Act), which was basically NCLB disguised as something new and improved. It was still a test-driven system, and it, too, has failed to deliver. Better test scores were the goal, but scores have not improved much, if at all, and the test-driven system has instead diminished the quality of education our kids are receiving.

Although the US spends more money per student than most other countries in the world, US students perform only slightly above average in reading and science, and they perform slightly below average in mathematics, according to results from an international exam. The outcome of that exam also showed no significant improvement or decline in reading since 2000, in math since 2003, and in science since 2006.[4]

The fact that the US spends so much money on education and yet has so little to show for it demonstrates that more money does not necessarily yield better test results, and it certainly doesn't equal a better learning experience for our kids. That's because learning can't and shouldn't be driven by standardized test scores. It was never meant to be.

Our kids come to us curious and wanting to learn; naturally, they learn best at their own pace and via engagement with the things *they* are actually interested in. A one-size-fits-all education isn't optimal for most kids because kids are people. They each have unique, God-given characteristics, gifts, and passions. It only makes sense that their educational journeys would be vast and varied and yet still be equal in value because people themselves are vast and varied and equal in value.

Deep down, I think most parents know this; we just aren't sure what to do about it. Since we've likely been told in both direct and indirect ways that we are not qualified to make these decisions, we abdicate that role to schools.

You Are Qualified

I'm here to tell you that you *are* qualified.

If you and I were sitting together on my front porch, and I asked you to share the ways you believe the system is failing our kids in general, I bet you could tell me. If we were talking specifically about *your* kids, I'm confident you could tell me much more. Why is that? Because you have a God-ordained role in your child's life.

When God created the family, he gave parents responsibility for the lives of their children. Not only do we love our kids more than anyone else does, we are also more invested in their futures. These are gifts that motivate us to be our children's biggest advocates. Even more than that, our role and responsibility as parents is a calling God has placed on our lives. I often tell parents that God doesn't call the qualified; he qualifies the called. In other words, if God has called you to be your child's parent, he will equip you for the task. He won't do it all at once, but he will supply what you need as you need it. This includes providing what your children need for their education.

Perhaps you're familiar with the so-called 10,000-hour rule. It states that 10,000 hours (on average) of "deliberate practice" are required to become an expert in a given field. Did you know that the average parent will devote 16,000 hours to their child by the time that child reaches the age of six? This makes the average parent an expert on their child right around the time that child is school age.

Consider this same metric in the context of the traditional school system. To reach the 16,000-hour mark with a child, a schoolteacher would have to have that child in his or her classroom six hours a day for all 180 days of the school year for fifteen years. And that's just to reach the point parents reach by the time the child is six.

So, yes, you absolutely have the freedom to question the system. You *are* in a position—a God-given position—to make decisions for your children that you believe are in their best interests.

More to Offer

While we are having that conversation, it might be helpful to look back at how the current educational system in the United States came into being in the first place, as it might explain what lies at the root of our concerns.

Most would consider Horace Mann the first great American advocate of public education, but his ideas actually originated in Prussia (the former Germany). I find it interesting that as a father, he clearly believed the concept of the taxpayer funded, compulsory educational system was good for the masses but not for his own children. When we have a better understanding of how and why the system was set up like it was, we get a clearer understanding of why it's not working and should have been restructured long ago.[5]

Here we are, over two decades into the twenty-first century, and we are still following an antiquated educational model that is plagued by a host of problems, including inequitable funding, teaching to test results, and politically motivated curriculum choices. In other words, the educational system is not designed around what works best for the individual child—*your* child.

Home education has so much more to offer than a classroom education. Not only can we customize our kids' learning, we can take the time to grow productive, healthy, stable adults who bring value to the world around them—and the world could use more of that! We can also better prepare them for an unknown future by equipping them with the skills required to navigate the uncharted territory of a rapidly changing world. Even twenty-one years ago, I could never have guessed that our five-year-old son would one day be in high demand as a software engineer, or that online sales or making YouTube videos would be a viable means of making a living.

If there is no way to know what our kids might one day do for a living, how in the world can we prepare them? It's a question I asked myself almost thirty years ago, and it became the catalyst for a paradigm shift in my perspective on education.

As I have walked out our home education journey with our eight kids and watched other families do the same, I've had the privilege of seeing the incredibly positive and encouraging outcomes of avoiding the one-size-fits-all approach. Doing so enabled me to embrace the adventure of an educational experience that has allowed our kids to become who they were uniquely made to be. However, in order to provide a more personalized education, I first had to let go of my preconceived ideas of what education *should* look like. I've done a lot of that kind of letting go over the years, which is part of why I can say with confidence that homeschooling is both effective and efficient.

If you ask a schoolteacher what makes for a good education, they will most likely state the following: low student-to-teacher ratio, good curriculum, and learning and teaching methods that work best for the child. In homeschooling, you get all of those things.

- **A low student-to-teacher ratio.** It's just you and your child.
- **Good curriculum.** You have the ability to customize the curriculum to your child's needs.
- **Learning and teaching methods that work best for the child.** You know your child best and can adapt your approach based on what helps your child engage in real learning.

All of this can be done in a fraction of the time required during a traditional school day.

There *is* one big hurdle most of us need to get over, and it's believing we have to know everything in order to give our kids a good education. This simply isn't true. No teacher has to know everything in order to teach your child, and neither do you. You just have to be tuned into your child and tuned into the God who made them. I love this statement I've heard attributed to author and veteran teacher John Taylor Gatto: "There are as many ways to educate as there are fingerprints." In other words, your children's education can be as unique as they are.

I heard someone say recently that education is not comprehensive; it's selective. There is no way to know everything about everything, so education is about making choices. When we send our kids to school, we make the decision to let someone else choose what our children will learn, and we really have no say in what that will or will not be.

It's time for a wake-up call. We have abdicated countless parental rights to the public school system for long enough. We need to be willing to ask the hard questions and put the system under the microscope. We need to step up, protect our children, and do what is best for *them*.

FACTS ABOUT THE PERFORMANCE OF HOME-EDUCATED STUDENTS

According to a National Home Education Research Institute summary of the latest research studies on home education, there are many compelling facts supporting the effectiveness of homeschooling.

Academic Performance

- Home-educated students score 15 to 30 percent above public school students on standardized academic achievement tests. A 2015 study found Black homeschool students scored 23 to 42 percent above Black public school students.
- Homeschool students' above-average scores on achievement tests were consistent regardless of household income or their parents' level of formal education.
- Degree of state control and regulation of homeschooling is not related to academic achievement.
- Home-educated students achieve above-average scores on college admissions tests, such as the SAT and ACT.
- Colleges and universities are increasingly recruiting homeschool students.

Social, Emotional, and Psychological Development

- Home-educated students consistently test above average on measures of social, emotional, and psychological development. This includes measures ranging from peer interaction and leadership skills to family cohesion and self-esteem.

- Homeschool students are actively engaged in social and educational activities—sports, scouting, volunteer work—with people other than family members.
- Adults who were educated at home are more politically tolerant than students educated in public school.

It's clear that homeschooling yields positive results that aren't based on parents knowing everything or on levels of funding or privilege. At its very core, the success of home education is parents who are warm, loving, and engaged parents who decide to take back what really belongs to them.

REAL-LIFE APPLICATION

1. What are some things you have questioned when it comes to your child's current educational experience?

2. Are you confident that you know your child better than anyone?

3. Do you believe that you are, in fact, qualified to be your child's best advocate and facilitate their education?

4. I shared some compelling facts about the outcome of homeschoolers. What did you find the most encouraging?

CHAPTER 4

Teaching through Your Child's Passion

Until Jake was twelve years old, he hated reading. He loved lots of other things, but language arts, in general, was his archnemesis. We regularly took him and his seven siblings to a large bookstore to choose any book they wanted. Darryl and I beamed with satisfaction as the kids proudly held the treasures they got to take home. Each time, Jake was the only one who walked away empty-handed because he said he couldn't find anything interesting.

Seriously? I couldn't even count the number of times I'd had to restrict myself from buying books I thought looked interesting, and this kid couldn't find a single book in the entire store that interested him? I truly couldn't relate, but I also knew that more than likely, all he needed was time—he would eventually find *something*. Yet as time wore on, I started to get nervous.

I'm definitely not one to force learning, but this was getting to be a bit much. At what point should I force the kid to get with the program? And yet every time I was tempted to apply the pressure, something inside of me said, "Just wait. Be patient."

Finally, it happened. During another bookstore visit when Jake was twelve, he walked up to me with a book in hand and asked if I would buy it for him. I could almost hear angels singing the "Hallelujah Chorus" as he handed it to me. I was on the edge of my seat, wondering what amazing literary work had finally grabbed our boy's attention.

I looked at the cover: C++. My first thought was, "That's not a very gripping title." I had no idea what this book was about.

"What *is* this?" I asked.

"A book on computer coding," he said.

My mind reeled. As I thumbed through the pages, I could only wonder who in their right mind would ever want to read a book like this. Of course, I said none of this out loud. The wheels in my homeschool mom brain were turning, and I began to think about how I could use this to his advantage as well as my own.

"I will buy you this book on one condition," I said. "You have to promise to read the whole thing from cover to cover."

Don't get me wrong; he was already doing some reading every day—reading I assigned out of a sheer sense of responsibility as a homeschooling parent. But I was really trying to avoid causing him to develop a complete hatred for it, so that assigned reading time was minimal. In making this deal, I figured the worst-case scenario was that C++ would buy me some required reading time that I didn't have to feel guilty about.

"I promise to read the whole thing," he said.

Guess what? He read the whole thing! Then, he read another book on computer science, and then another. Four years later, Jake started college at age sixteen, and he is now a successful software engineer. Today, he tells me that age twelve was a defining time in his life. He suddenly *knew* he wanted to be a computer programmer. From that moment on, it was this passion that drove his desire to learn. Naturally, it involved more reading and writing.

To be clear, Darryl and I are not tech savvy. Neither of us has a computer science background. To pursue his dream, Jake had to eventually do some serious upper-level math. I could help him only until about seventh grade. His dad could help him a little beyond that, but our eventual inability to help him ended up not mattering. Once Jake zeroed in on his goal, nothing stopped him. He found resources online to help him when he got stuck on a math problem. In fact, he seemed to take sheer delight in overcoming and solving complicated equations on his own.

Reading and writing never became a passion for Jake, but his passion for computer coding drove him to learn more *about* reading and writing. Still, he did minimal work in formal language arts over the next four years. It felt a little like we were limping along, with my goal simply being not to extinguish his drive to become a software engineer.

Then came the day when Jake took the entrance exams at the local community college. I was sweating bullets. This was the moment of reckoning. I felt certain I would find out what a failure I really was.

"So? How did the English entrance exam go?" I asked later.

"Oh, I aced it," Jake said absentmindedly.

"Excuse me? How?" I was trying not to sound too shocked, but we were both aware of his lack of enthusiasm for language arts.

"Mom, you taught us how to speak well at home," he said. (It's true, I am a proud member of the grammar police.) "And you made me write summaries of what I read every day. That's pretty much all I needed to know."

Once again, I heard angels singing the "Hallelujah Chorus."

Jake's first quarter of college landed him in a rigorous English/history class that required him to write exceptionally involved term papers. I asked him if I could read the first one he completed, and I honestly couldn't believe he had written it. It was so well done. I had no idea he could write like that. I don't think *he* had any idea he could write like that. What made the difference? His passion was driving him.

The Connection between Interests and Learning

I love to tell this story about Jake because it so clearly demonstrates the powerful connection between interest and learning. This is how real learning happens all along the way—from the very beginning, not just when kids discover what they want to do for a career. This is why it's crucial that we allow them time to follow their interests. This eventually leads kids to discover their unique giftings, and it teaches them the joy of working with purpose.

Early on, we recognized that Jake loved trying to figure out how things worked. It started when he was less than two and would lay his head on the floor while pushing his fire truck back and forth, staring at the turning wheels for long periods of time. We could almost see the wheels turning in his mind as he tried to figure out how the wheels on the fire truck worked.

When Jake was four, my coffee grinder broke. Instead of throwing it away, I asked him if he could try to fix it. It was headed to the trash, so what harm could there be in letting him tinker with it? Somehow, he managed to get it working again. We made a *big* deal out of it. We told his siblings and our friends and watched Jake's face light up with pride and growing confidence that no amount of forced learning could match. We were throwing fuel on the fire of his love for learning.

If you have ever started a campfire or a wood fire in a fireplace, you know kindling is important to get the fire started. But kindling and wood also need to be carefully arranged so that oxygen can flow and feed the flames. By being present and aware as a parent, you are able to provide the equivalent of oxygen to your child's fire for learning. You do that by encouraging the conditions for success. You watch for indicators that the fire might go out, and then, slowly and carefully, give it encouragement to keep burning. Sometimes that involves blowing gently to fan the flames. What you *don't* want to do is blow too much too soon or load on too much heavy wood, because then, the flames will most certainly be snuffed out. Instead, you create an environment that allows a small spark to eventually turn into a roaring fire. You don't know when the spark will happen, but when it does, you are watching and ready to encourage it.

Curiosity sparks interest, and interest sparks learning. What if I had insisted on a results-driven outcome in Jake's education? Would he have discovered what he was passionate about so early in life? I doubt it. As I noted earlier, we encouraged Jake toward a love of learning from the time he was very young, as we did for all of our kids. I have watched all of them cycle in and out of countless interests. Some lasted only a matter of hours, others lasted days and weeks, and a few became lifelong passions.

It's important to understand that a child's interest doesn't have to turn into a passion or a career in order to have educational value. In fact, the opposite is true. When we allow our kids to follow what interests them for as long as it holds their attention, we send a clear message that their interests have value—that message gives them the courage to experiment and feeds their love of learning. It also makes them feel valued, which, in turn, increases their confidence. We encourage a love of learning by acknowledging that their ideas are worth pursuing.

A Harmony of Approaches

If all of this is true, you might be wondering what, specifically, your involvement is in this process. I like to describe the most effective and efficient education as a harmony of both directed and self-directed learning. This makes all the difference in terms of the amount of time we, as parents, have to spend being directly involved in our kids' education.

My view is that we can focus the bulk of our hands-on energy and time on the basics: developing reading, writing, and math skills. Beyond that, we can trust our kids to eventually find their own way to their ultimate career path by self-educating through their interests. This doesn't mean we aren't involved in *any* of their self-education, but our role is more that of an observer and facilitator.

As parents who are observing our kids and facilitating their education, we can keep our finger on the pulse of what's engaging them that day or week or month and flex with it. The point isn't that they have to dive deeply into every subject, but rather that they make their way to the subjects that engage them and are allowed time to pursue them.

Author C. S. Lewis said, "The greatest service we can do to education today is to teach fewer subjects. No one has time to do more than a very few things well before he is twenty, and when we force a boy to be a mediocrity in a dozen subjects, we destroy his standards, perhaps for life."[1] When our kids own what they are doing and are allowed to see it through to the end—the end they choose—they have the opportunity to do things well.

This trust in our children flies in the face of all we have been taught about educating them—specifically, that we should entrust that role to someone else. Author and educator John Holt said, "To trust children we must first learn to trust ourselves . . . and most of us were taught as children that we could not be trusted."[2]

This is true. Very few of us feel qualified to teach our kids because we have been sent a clear message that parents don't know what's really important when it comes to learning or education. When we were students, we were told what to learn and when to learn it, so it's the only educational model we know. And yet, how many of us actually remember most of what we learned in school? What *do* we remember? Most likely, what we remember are the things we were interested in and the things we find necessary in adulthood. So why are we trying to force that same kind of education on our kids?

Here's another statement I resonate with from educator John Holt:

> We can best help children learn, not by deciding what we think they should learn and thinking of ingenious ways to teach it to them, but by making the world, as far as we can, accessible to them, paying serious attention to what *they* do, answering their questions—if they have any—and helping them explore the things they are most interested in.[3]

The most effective and efficient path to helping our kids find their unique giftings and passions is to create an environment that fosters self-led learning through encouraging experiences, exploration, and experiments. Self-directed learning does not mean no adult involvement. It means no adult forcing or controlling.

There is only one problem: this requires us to let go and trust, approaching education with an open heart and mind, one that respects our children's God-given curiosity and desire to learn. It requires suppressing our need to micromanage their education and refusing to think of our kids as projects we have to coerce into conformity with a very narrow plan.

We seem to have this picture in our minds that learning is a strictly linear process. In other words, we must learn A before we learn B. However, Math is about the only subject that actually follows this model. For almost everything else, learning is made up of networks—a collection of experiences, explorations, and experiments. Eventually, the networks start connecting, and that's when all kinds of great things start happening—but first, we have to let go and trust.

We also have to be patient. We have to be students of our kids, not in the sense that we hover over them, but in the sense that we are tuned into them. What does that look like? A great analogy is growing a garden. If you haven't grown a garden, you've likely grown a seed, and you'll still be able to get the idea.

I grew a large garden several years in a row, but one year, I had a noticeably large harvest. It was so much more than previous years that I had to ask myself what I had done differently. It didn't take me long to figure it out.

That year, I went into the garden every day, not usually for extended periods of time (unless needed), but consistently. I spent whatever time was necessary that day to check on each of the plants. I inspected for bugs, checked to see which ones needed water, and looked for weeds or any other sign indicating my plants were at risk. What made the difference that year was consistency. I consistently created the healthiest environment possible so my garden could flourish.

I did the same thing with my kids. Because they were home with me, I could easily check in with them at opportune times—sometimes by having a conversation and other times by simply watching their responses to daily responsibilities, play, interests, bookwork, or relationships.

Are you beginning to see the difference between what we've been taught is "education" and how kids really learn? Here is how educator and author Ken Robinson described the change that needs to take place in how we approach education:

> We have to go from what is essentially an industrial model of education, a manufacturing model, which is based on linearity and conformity and batching people. We have to move to a model that is based more on principles of agriculture. We have to recognize that human flourishing is not a mechanical process; it's an organic process. And you cannot predict the outcome of human development. All you can do, like a farmer, is create the conditions under which they will begin to flourish.[4]

Human flourishing seems like a much more helpful way to approach education and learning. Most importantly, it's also a much more helpful and wholesome mindset from which to help little human beings grow.

I've spent countless hours watching my kids' behavior, attitudes, interests, strengths, weaknesses, successes, and failures through all stages of childhood. I learned so much about who they are as persons and how I could best help them in different seasons of their lives. Sometimes, that meant letting them struggle so they could develop resilience. Other times, it meant helping them find resources that would give them the boost of encouragement and support they needed. This is what I was referring to earlier when I said our role is that of an observer and facilitator.

This is the role I was fulfilling when I handed four-year-old Jake that coffee grinder. It was the role I was fulfilling when, at fourteen, he told us he wanted to build a computer. We were raising eight kids on one income, so money wasn't exactly easy to come by, but Jake had earned money doing odd jobs for our neighbors and wanted to pay for it himself. All I had to do was place the order for the parts. To be honest, I was nervous for him. I didn't want him to end up losing money by ordering the wrong parts. I really wanted him to be successful, but there was no way I could ensure that would happen because neither my husband nor I knew anything about computers. Darryl said we should trust Jake, so I ordered the parts on the list he gave me. As it turned out, Jake's list was thorough and accurate. He not only built his computer, but it is still working beautifully over twelve years later and is being used by one of his younger siblings.

Do you see what happened in this situation? The project was driven entirely by Jake's interest in computers: researching, list making, taking the initiative to talk with his dad and me about it, investing his own hard-earned money, and seeing the project to completion. He took risks and overcame obstacles. The fact that it was a success was secondary to the fact that Jake was firing on all cylinders when it came to learning.

Something similar happened with Ben, though the

process was completely different. Ben has always been a role player. When he was two, he became obsessed with Thomas the Tank Engine. He donned a train engineer's outfit for two years straight and spent most of his days playing the part. Then he became consumed with bull riding and cowboys. I think that lasted four or five years. Because he was home, Ben could consume all the information he wanted about his obsessions, along with the topics that stemmed from them. He became a lover of history and still is. He was inspired to read and write *because* he loved history. One of the topics he studied was explorers. When he got into high school geometry, he excelled at it because instead of just seeing shapes, measurements, and equations in a math problem, he envisioned himself as an explorer. In other words, his passion for role playing helped him with geometry.

This is why it's absolutely crucial to give our kids time and space to follow their interests. Not only does it eventually lead to the discovery of their unique passions, gifts, and talents, it also helps them more easily learn how they learn. It was natural for Ben to resort to role-playing because he had been allowed to fully develop that interest. At home, he wasn't mocked or made fun of for it; instead, he was encouraged, and therefore, he wasn't ashamed to use it later on for higher learning.

Our daughter, Jenna, has always had a passion for words. She used to read the dictionary for *fun*. Her younger siblings would gather around her on the couch while she read new words and their meanings aloud. Her passion ignited learning in her siblings and passed on a better vocabulary to them as well.

We used to get together with another homeschooling family, and two of their boys loved to tease our girls. Jenna's response was to write what she called, "dictionary letters" in which she essentially "roasted" them (in fun) with words they had never heard and would have to look up. There was a competitive feel to the whole thing that drove yet another facet of learning. This evolved into sharpening her debate skills.

Today, Jenna is a mom who influences her community of peers with intelligent, well-articulated arguments for and against important issues faced by the current generation of moms. She often encourages them by asking relevant questions and approaching difficult topics with both logic and tenderness.

The most effective form of learning educates the *whole* person, but it doesn't happen overnight. It happens by sowing one tiny seed at a time, then watering, feeding, nurturing, and covering it all in prayer. No one forces a garden to grow. Instead, we work with what God has given us and follow his lead. We don't plant delicate seeds when there is still danger of frost. We don't water when it's already rained. We pay attention to keeping a balance of all the conditions that will encourage the healthiest growth. It's not mechanical; it's organic.

Children are born with an enthusiasm for learning, especially when it comes to things they find fascinating. They have a sense of adventure and fearlessness most adults have outgrown. They will wholeheartedly dive into whatever captures their interest, and learning happens effectively, efficiently, and multi-dimensionally as a result.

I believe this is a gift from God. It is meant to be a blessing—not just for children, but for us as parents. If we respect and honor this gift, homeschooling becomes both doable and enjoyable for the whole family. It becomes a shared experience that lends itself not only to growing healthy, productive adults, but also strong, cohesive families that provide foundational support for each other throughout the rest of their lives.

REAL-LIFE APPLICATION

1. In what ways do you see your child engaging in self-directed learning? What do they seem passionate about?

2. In what ways do you feel you need to direct your child's learning? In other words, what do you believe is important for them to be learning at this particular time?

3. Reflect on this quote from chapter 4: C. S. Lewis said, "The greatest service we can do to education today is to teach fewer subjects. No one has time to do more than a very few things well before he is twenty, and when we force a boy to be mediocre in a dozen subjects, we destroy his standards, perhaps for life."

4. What do you think are the most important skills your child should master for life?

5. If you haven't already, spend some time being a student of your child and make notes on what you observe.

6. Are there ways you could encourage a more natural learning process for your child?

CHAPTER 5

Who's Driving the Bus?

Nurturing Independent Learners

In the movie *The Princess Bride*, a self-important villain named Vizzini uses the word "inconceivable" multiple times. At one point, Inigo Montoya, our hero, looks at him and says, "You keep using that word. I do not think it means what you think it means."

I've had similar thoughts after seeing people's reactions when I tell them I homeschooled eight kids. I can see the wheels turning as they try to envision what that actually looks like in everyday life. I imagine they see me as a schoolmarm who runs her household with a whip in one hand and her lesson planner in the other. She maintains a tight ship and has all her ducks in a row. She may even blow the hearty whistle Baron von Trapp used in *The Sound of Music* to get his children lined up neatly by age, complete with matching outfits. At the very least, they must think I have a holy amount of patience because, as we all know, no one with a normal amount of patience would ever attempt to homeschool eight kids.

Nothing could be farther from the truth. Our homeschooling days looked very little like people probably thought they did—and I'm glad for it. What made homeschooling so doable with that many kids was that we encouraged independent learning from the very beginning.

Of course, when the kids were too young to read or write, it was necessary for me to sit down with them, walk them through their short reading lessons, and teach them how to write their letters and numbers. Once they were able to do that on their own, we moved into using a couple of workbooks every day. They knew the routine: after morning chores and breakfast, it was time to sit down and do a certain number of pages in their workbooks. I was available if they got stuck or needed help, but I encouraged them to work as independently as possible.

Looking back, it was a rather simple approach, but you have to remember that there was no internet when we started homeschooling. I had no one and nothing to compare it to— no Pinterest boards, no Instagram feeds, no Facebook.

Oh, sure, there was the occasional encounter with the overachieving homeschool mom who found it necessary to share all of the amazing projects and field trips she arranged for her family. But most of the time, I was left to myself to find a rhythm that worked for our family. That rhythm encouraged independence and simplicity. It seemed to me that my kids were innately smart, and what they needed from me was to create an environment that did two things: sent a message that I thought they were smart and could handle much of their learning on their own, and gave them lots of time, space, and respect for their own learning timetables.

When I see the creativity with which some parents homeschool now, especially in the early years, I have mixed emotions. On one hand, I think about how fun their ideas look and how we might have enjoyed that back in the day. On the other hand, I empathize with the heavy pressure homeschooling parents today feel to perform. I truly enjoyed our homeschool days—most of them, anyway—and my kids.

Don't get me wrong; I never thought the overachieving homeschool mom was doing anything detrimental to her children. In fact, I honestly grew to respect each mom's God-given instincts concerning her children. I have seen over and over again that it's not necessary or helpful to let our differences create bitter competition. I agree with educator John Taylor Gatto, who said, "There isn't a right way to become educated. There are as many ways as fingerprints!"[1]

My simple approach worked for our family. In fact, every time I tried to add much more to it or make significant changes, it seemed to either backfire on me or work only in the short term. Over time, I concluded that independent learning and simplicity were better for us.

Encourage Ownership

When Luke was seventeen, he took a chemistry class at a local high school. The teacher was a veteran educator about to retire. At the start of the school year, he announced that he was tired—tired of teaching, and tired of grading papers. He apologized up front and told the students they would be hitting only the highlights of chemistry throughout that school year.

To this day, Luke tells me it was one of his favorite classes. Because he wasn't overwhelmed with too much information, he had room to wonder and ask questions. This led him to dive into research to figure out the answers.

Even though he doesn't have a career that involves chemistry, Luke still loves to read about it just for fun, and he has a solid foundation in chemistry should he ever need to draw on it.

Whether our kids were engaged in directed learning or interest-led learning, I let them be responsible for as much as they could be. Some might call it a mom survival tactic, but it was certainly one of the most beneficial things I ever did. It looked different for each child and at various age levels, but it really came down to simply ownership.

When I suggest my kids learn about something, it's *my* idea. In their minds, that means it belongs to me. However, when they find something interesting and take responsibility for it, it's *their* idea. They own it. Then they are invested in learning in ways I could never make happen by forcing my ideas on them. When they self-educate, their whole being is involved, and they are firing on all cylinders. John Holt said, "Children are not only extremely good at learning; they are much better at it than we are."[2] So it's actually very safe, effective, and efficient to encourage our kids to take ownership of their education.

One of the ways I encouraged ownership during our kids' directed learning time was by noting when they struggled. If a particular subject wasn't going well, we'd have a conversation about why they thought it wasn't going well. Kids are amazingly intuitive. If you ask them enough questions, they can tell you what the problem is.

"What do you think the directions are telling you to do?"

"What do you think is causing you grief?"

"Do you think there is a way to overcome it?"

"Do you think you might need to learn it a different way?"

"How can I help?"

"Do you think you just need a break and you can go back to it after that?"

By asking them questions, I wasn't abdicating my role as a parent, but rather involving them by asking for their input. By inviting them into the conversation, I was encouraging ownership and a certain amount of independence. This happened more and more as the kids grew older.

Have the Right Expectations

Not every parent takes the same approach, but in the early years, most parents tend to lean toward one of two different methods: either expecting too much or expecting too little from their kids. I've seen parents who do things for their littles that the littles could easily be encouraged to do for themselves, and I've seen parents who expect their littles to act like adults and are irritated when they don't. On any given day, a parent may alternate between these two approaches, depending on the parent's mood or level of energy, but what children need is consistency. The only way to effectively nurture independent learning is to have an idea of where your kids are at developmentally. And as I said earlier, you don't have to have a degree to do that; you just need to be tuned into your child.

So, what does this look like? Honestly, it looks different at different age levels.

For instance, you instinctively know that a three-month-old isn't even close to being ready to learn to walk. You don't think about trying to teach them before they seem ready; you just wait patiently until they start to pull themselves up and maybe even begin to let go of support and try to take a step or two on their own. These are indications that they are ready. At this point, most parents encourage their child to try walking by placing themselves just a little way away from the child and holding out their arms while cheering them on. If the child doesn't try, or tries and then falls down, the parents don't get upset. They simply encourage their child to try again or wait for the next time the child wants to make another attempt.

We can apply this same method throughout the toddler, preschool, and early elementary years. The problem comes when we are not tuned into our child and expect either too much or too little. The easiest way to be tuned into our child is to be with them—to spend time with them. When young children spend the bulk of their day in the care of warm, loving, engaged parents, they quickly grow in confidence and healthy independence.

In the early years (preschool through early elementary school), kids have a deep need for routine. Regular eating and sleeping times ground them and help them feel secure. When these needs are met, they can more easily get down to the business of being kids and learning in ways that come naturally.

A healthy family life filled with simple daily activities is a perfect setting for young children to thrive in and for us to recognize opportunities to encourage independence. I have noticed that just when I'm beginning to feel tired of doing something for my child, my child is often ready to do that thing for themselves. This isn't always the case, but it's a little red flag I try to pay attention to.

Do the Right Amount for the Season You're In

I have also learned that things don't go as well when we try to do too much in a day or are distracted. Time and again, I had to set aside my perfectionistic tendencies and slow down to the pace my child needed. If we are going to encourage independence at opportune times, we have to be willing to adapt to our child's pace over and over again.

Throughout our simple days, the goal is to include our little ones as much as we can, especially when they show an interest in something. When our toddlers want to take things out of the dishwasher while we are unloading it, that's the beginning of teaching them how to eventually unload it by themselves. But it starts by encouraging their interest when they show it. We can also invite them into many of the everyday things we already have to do. They can pretend to fold laundry from a very early age and then learn to fold the simpler things, such as washcloths. Over time, this morphs into doing the laundry on their own.

We take them to the grocery store, have conversations about what we are shopping for, and let them get something off the shelf and put it in the cart. We teach them how to respond appropriately when people stop and talk to them or when they're talking with the cashier.

The older they get, the more we explain, and the more they can help. We encourage them to button or zip their own coats, put on their own shoes, make their own beds. They don't have to do any of this perfectly; we just keep encouraging as much independence as possible.

As we live out our days with our kids alongside us, they become increasingly confident and independent. This automatically begins to spill over into any bookwork they do as they move into the school years, and that makes a world of difference when it comes to the amount of time and energy that is required of us. Don't get me wrong; home educating our kids does require time and energy, but it's far less overwhelming when we nurture independent learners.

By the time the elementary years rolled around, our kids were typically used to the routine. I'm not saying they never complained or never dragged their feet, but they knew that when all was said and done, their responsibilities were not optional. At that point, they were reading, writing, and doing basic math on their own with help from me whenever they asked for or needed it. In the meantime, I might be busy feeding a baby, sorting a load of laundry, reading to a toddler, or directing children who were lagging behind on their chores.

When I had six kids aged nine and under, most of our days were spent just keeping some semblance of order in our home, diapers changed, and toddlers directed. I involved all of our older kids in that process. I'll admit that my main motive was to keep the house from falling down around us. I knew the kids were learning something, but I had no idea what a solid foundation I was laying for them simply by involving them in the everyday practicalities of family life.

At one point, I realized I was feeling guilty at the end of every week for completing only three days of bookwork. I kept shooting for four to five, but it seemed like I had to be an ogre to make that happen, and I simply wasn't willing to do that. God reminded me that this was the season of life we were in, and he was sovereign over it. I had to trust him. So I settled into three days a week for that season. Twenty-five years later, I can say it made no difference in my children's "success." In fact, I would say it was actually beneficial.

You see, as my kids were simply living their daily lives, they were learning responsibility, teamwork, communication, how to be others-oriented, a solid work ethic, and much more. They each felt like an important and vital part of our family, not only loved and wanted but *needed*. They were part of something bigger than themselves and that grew their confidence, which, in turn, naturally nurtured their independence. They believed they had important things to do because the most important people in their world were depending on them.

Transitioning to Even Greater Independence

In our culture, high school is a time when kids are expected to step into that phase of transition, becoming more adult than child. They are typically ready for more complex learning, and their brains are better able to absorb information and process it in an adult way. Their ability to reason is (we hope) kicking in, and they become capable of a broader form of thinking.

With that in mind, I began preparing our kids for high school while they were still in middle school. I let each one of them know that things would change when they entered high school. I would be expecting them to fully own their education. I would be less involved and do more coaching from the sidelines. Together, we would look at the credits they needed to graduate and then talk about how they wanted to get those credits. For instance, to meet a biology credit, we would consider several options: a textbook, a DVD course, an online class, a real-life class, or a more hands-on experiential approach. I let them choose. In our state, the requirement to earn a high school credit was 170 hours, so we used that as a guideline. They were responsible to be sure they put in those hours or completed a course or textbook.

They were also responsible for writing a monthly progress report including a brief overview of what they covered in each subject of study. I encouraged courses that were self-checking or self-grading. I wanted them to feel like they were driving the bus, so-to-speak. That put more of the burden on them than on me.

Because I let them know my expectations ahead of time and made this transition a significant rite of passage rather than a burden, they were actually excited about going into high school. Some of them felt a certain amount of pressure, but it was a good kind of pressure and completely age appropriate. I assured them I was there to encourage them and help them overcome obstacles, but when each one of them walked across that stage and was handed their diploma, they could be proud because it was *their* accomplishment, not mine.

Every single one of them rose to the occasion and proudly graduated. Knowing that this was the result of their own work, that diploma really meant something to every one of them. They owned the process, and they truly earned it.

1. Do you believe your expectations of your child are reasonable?

2. Are there subjects or areas of learning where your child shows ownership?

3. In what ways could you encourage more ownership?

4. In this chapter, I talk about being tuned in to your child. There are things we don't know because our children are always growing and changing, but there are plenty of things we do know. Make a list of things you know about your child.

5. Go through the list you just made and determine whether you are expecting too much or too little both in schoolwork and everyday life. (Look up age-appropriate chores, for example.)

6. Are there ways you can involve your child more in your daily activities?

7. What season of life are you in, and how might that affect your approach to homeschooling?

CHAPTER 6

Educating for Life, Not Just Graduation

From the first moment we hold our child in our arms, something inside us changes forever. We become far less consumed with our own needs and, instead, are focused on the well-being of this tiny, helpless person who now belongs to us forever. Never has anyone depended so heavily on us for every little thing. We are completely responsible to keep this little human alive and growing.

At first, their dependency can feel overwhelming, but as time passes, we settle a little more comfortably into our role as a parent. It isn't long before our children are school age, and we begin to think more about how to prepare them for the future. Their education is one of the first things we consider.

When I reached this point as a young mom, I knew I wanted to homeschool, but how in the world could I know what my kids needed to know for a future I simply could not see? What would the job market look like in the future? How would I know what they needed in order to do what God had called them to do? How could I be sure they didn't miss anything important?

At the time, I felt both inadequate and keenly aware that I couldn't possibly figure all of this out. But I also realized that not even a fully trained and experienced teacher could do that. There were things they knew that I didn't, but when all was said and done, I also knew that no amount of knowledge could compare with the deep love, ongoing concern, and lifetime investment I had in my own children and their future. As their mom, I was willing to move heaven and earth to overcome whatever obstacles we might face in order to give them a childhood and an education uniquely tailored to them.

Worthy Goals

Instead of fretting over methods and curriculum, I began with the end in mind: equipping my kids for adult life. What skills might my kids need in order to be able to navigate the world well? What tools could I give them that would best enable them to teach themselves? If they had these life skills and knew how to teach themselves, it seemed to me that they would likely be able to enter any field they chose. Now, looking back over more than two decades, I can say that our homeschooling was successful. Each of our kids is well-equipped with these life skills, which have served them well. But getting to this point required me to continue to view their education with the end in mind. I didn't want my kids faltering well into their twenties and early thirties, as so many young people are doing today.

In his book *Marching Off the Map*, Tim Elmore notes that we have "begun to witness a strange paradox in our young: the extinction of childlikeness and the extension of childishness. Since they are exposed to so much adult information so early in their lives, they can prematurely lose their sense of innocence, their sense of wonder, and their sense of trust."[1] I didn't want this to happen to my kids.

Before the internet dawned and all of this unraveled before us, my gut instinct as a mom told me that it was crucial for kids to have a healthy, normal childhood filled with beauty, wonder, and as much innocence as possible. I considered it my calling and my duty to try and make that happen. I didn't know it at the time, but I've since learned that these goals were worthy. Not only did this approach give my kids great childhood memories, it also allowed for generous amounts of play, especially in the early years, which laid a firm foundation for higher learning. (We'll talk more about this in chapter 8.)

Those precious years of wonder and innocence are cut terribly short for a child who begins attending school at age five or six. Suddenly, pressure to perform extinguishes their childlikeness. As parents, we can mistakenly believe that educating earlier is better and will give our kids an edge, helping them get ahead; instead, it often holds them back and can lead to the "extension of childishness."

The Best Parenting Manual

I've heard it said that children don't come with a manual, but as Christian parents, we have something far greater: a direct connection with their Creator. Who knows better what our kids need than the One who created them? But how do we access the valuable information we need?

God gave us the gift of relationship with him, the Holy Spirit as our counselor, and his Word as our guide. The Bible has many things to say about children. Here a few:

- Children are a blessing (Psalm 127:3; Matthew 18:10).
- Children need to be trained (Proverbs 22:6).
- Children need faith passed down to them (Ephesians 6:1–4; Deuteronomy 6:1–3).
- Children must be taught wisdom (Proverbs 2:1–6).

Since God wants to give our kids and us a future and a hope (Jeremiah 29:11), it stands to reason that he intends for us to raise and educate our kids not just for graduation but for life. Life is complex and unpredictable, and kids need an education that equips them to handle that. We can't merely fill their heads with information and expect that they will be prepared to handle whatever comes their way. Therein lies the problem with ceding our kids' education to the powers that be. They don't know our kids like we do. They don't love them like we do. They are not even remotely invested in their futures. And yet they determine how our children will spend the bulk of every weekday—for twelve years.

We all want our kids to have a good education, but we err when we think of education as being "neutral." Education is *never* neutral.

Education is discipleship.

Discipleship is rooted in relationship.

Relationships take time.

This is why having our kids with us for the bulk of the day is so important and sharing life together so effective in preparing our kids for real life. Family life is not only a great teacher; it's something we have to navigate on a daily basis, so it makes sense that we can simply and readily use it to prepare our kids for the future. As they become adept at navigating everyday life, they also become problem solvers and critical thinkers.

Building Life Skills

An increasing number of high school graduates lack some foundational skills they need to succeed. Even though they may get good grades, understand upper-level math, and test well, they lack the so-called "soft skills" that enable them to collaborate with a team and perform well in their chosen fields.

What are soft skills? Here are some examples:

- Communication
- Problem-solving
- Leadership
- Teamwork
- Emotional intelligence
- Adaptability
- Work ethic

How in the world do we teach soft skills? It's simple.

Every single one of these skills can be effectively taught through everyday life in a family because every one of them is used in the home setting. Here's just one example of how learning soft skills has played out in our family.

With ten people eating three times a day, it was a crisis when the dishwasher broke down, which happened frequently. We lived far out in the country, so the repairman came to our area only once a week. The kids did all the dishes, so this meant they would be washing and drying everything by hand. Because the first repair visit was usually an evaluation followed by ordering parts, in all likelihood, the kids would be doing everything by hand for a minimum of ten to fourteen days. Most people would say this was inconvenient (and it was), but for us, it was a call to action. It was motivation because you can bet that my kids thought it through and knew what was at stake.

I invited any child who was interested in helping solve our dilemma onto the scene and had them look things over. We talked about what was possibly going wrong with the dishwasher, and I asked for potential solutions. During that process, I asked questions, and we bounced ideas off each other. Since kids tend to be competitive (especially boys), there was a kind of iron-sharpening-iron dynamic as they each tried to one-up each other with creative solutions. Inevitably, one or two led the charge, and the others followed. They dove in and started experimenting. Sometimes they could fix it, and sometimes we all arrived at the conclusion that we needed professional help.

Throughout that process, the kids had to use multiple soft skills—problem-solving, leadership, teamwork, emotional intelligence, adaptability, and work ethic. All that was required of me was simply to recognize the teaching opportunity, invite them into it, and engage with them throughout. Not every kid responded to the invitation, and not everyone engaged completely or for the duration, but I offered and encouraged engagement. They felt valued because I demonstrated my belief that they were quite possibly smart enough to solve the problem, and they rose to the occasion because they wanted to live up to my belief in them.

None of this required me to purchase a curriculum, create a lesson plan, or grade papers. It was a real-life problem, like the ones we face every day as adults. I was not just equipping our kids to deal with a dishwasher breaking down, I was helping them practice interpersonal or soft skills through face-to-face collaboration, problem-solving, and communication. Life hands us inconveniences and struggles, but almost every one of them has the potential to help us grow—*if* we take the time to recognize the opportunity and are willing to put forth the effort.

A Long-Term Investment

Did you catch the part about taking time? We have to be willing to slow down and invest wisely, because here's the thing: kids are a long-term investment. In the business world, a long-term investment is one that appears on the asset side of a company's balance sheet. It represents money the company has spent on things such as stocks, bonds, real estate, and cash.[2] In other words, even though it's spending, when someone is looking at the value of a company, a long-term investment counts as a plus, not a minus. While it's true that investing in our kids costs us something—we have to "spend" time and attention—we can count it as a plus, not minus. It's a long-term investment that adds a lifetime of value. This is why the Bible calls children a blessing and encourages us to invest wisely.

So what does this mean? What will our kids need to be able to do?

They will need to be able to have a relationship with God—without us.

They will need to be able to nurture other healthy relationships—without us.

They will need to be able to discern which resources and skills they need in a given situation—without us.

They will need to be able to research and learn—without us.

They will need to be able to arrange their work, make a plan, execute it, and reverse engineer it if necessary—without us.

They will need to be able to fall, get up, and start again—without us.

In short, they will need to be *whole* and *independent* human beings.

It's a long-term process that requires us to walk alongside them faithfully day in and day out, not micromanaging but discerning when to slow down, when to turn a corner, and when to let them take the lead. In order to give our kids a well-rounded education, we need to help them slowly but progressively *own* every aspect of their lives—and family life is the optimal place for that to happen.

At the Center

If you are just beginning this journey of home education, you will certainly have to make adjustments to your daily schedule, but let a healthy family life be at the center. In other words, the goal is for school to revolve around family and home life, not for family and home life to revolve around school.

Part of building a strong and cohesive family life is simply doing all the routine life management things. We have homes to maintain, meals to prepare, yards to tend. Some of us work outside the home. Depending on our family's priorities and needs, we can adjust homeschooling to fit our lifestyle and the season of life in which we find ourselves. And guess what? Our kids will be learning *through all of it*. Family life lends itself to lessons and preparation that could never be achieved the same way anywhere else. Every day, there is potential for conflict, obstacles that require teamwork to overcome, problems that need to be solved, work that needs to be done, and words that need to be communicated effectively.

Just as exercising at the gym helps develop the muscles in the body, family life gives our kids a workout that grows their character. Here is how author Tim Elmore described such opportunities:

It is in waiting that I build patience.

It is in face-to-face collaboration that I build inter-personal skills.

It is in attempting risky ventures that I build courage.

It is in struggling that I build perseverance.

It is in boredom that I have margins to imagine and think creatively.

It is in challenging labor that I build an appreciation for a strong work ethic.[3]

I'll give you fair warning: your kids aren't necessarily going to like or appreciate these lessons while they are learning them, but this is where we have to put on our big girl and big boy parenting pants. Or, in my case, my big girl gardening gloves.

I already mentioned that I had a large garden for several years when the kids were growing up. It wasn't just large; it was massive—seventy-five feet by one hundred feet—and for some reason, I felt the need to plant every square inch of it. I guess I figured if I didn't, weeds would grow there instead, which seemed counterproductive.

I spent a lot of time in that garden, and so did my kids. I made it a point to not go out there alone. Every time I went out, I grabbed one or two or more kids, and we worked together weeding, watering, or doing whatever needed to be done. Some days, it was pure torture—and I don't mean the work. I mean the howling and complaining. The more they complained, the longer I made them stay at it, sometimes long after the rest of us were finished.

But working in that garden also taught our kids many life lessons they still talk about today. An added bonus is that they now have stories to tell their kids about how hard they worked in the blazing sun on a garden that was far bigger than we needed. But more than that, they built a frame of reference for life in that garden because we had so many great conversations while we worked, about everything from the value of work to God's creation, relationships, teamwork, giftings, and so much more. It was a great way to get a peek into my kids' hearts and see where they were physically, mentally, emotionally, and spiritually. The garden was as much about relationships as anything else.

In home educating and preparing our kids for life, relationships are key. The first thing we need when we're building a relationship is time. The beauty of not sending our kids away for seven to eight hours a day is it gives us the ability to build stronger relationships, but we have to be intentional.

By building strong, healthy relationships with our kids, we give them a strong foundation from which to grow and learn. In her book, *Five to Thrive*, educational psychologist Dr. Kathy Koch reveals that security is the most basic core need of any human being. "Establishing and maintaining security is vital," she writes. "We need it so we'll take risks and grow. And, without it, healthy and lasting identity, belonging, purpose, and competence are not possible."[4]

God created family. It was a good plan, and it's still a good plan. It's not just about teaching and training our kids; it's about sharing life, building a life that centers around and is patterned after the redemption and restoration that can only come from knowing God. Family is the place where we can be fully known and truly loved. I love how author and pastor Tim Keller describes what that means:

> To be loved but not known is comforting but superficial. To be known and not loved is our greatest fear. But to be fully known and truly loved is, well, a lot like being loved by God. It is what we need more than anything. It liberates us from pretense, humbles us out of our self-righteousness, and fortifies us for any difficulty life can throw at us.[5]

Loving our children well is the greatest gift we will ever give them. None of us are perfect at this, but if we are willing to pour ourselves into our children, these blessings from God, his grace overflows, and he uses us to grow children who will truly make a difference in this world.

REAL-LIFE APPLICATION

1. What do you think are the most important life skills your child should master before fully launching into adult life?

2. How would you describe a healthy, functioning adult?

3. What kind of person do you hope your child will be? In other words, what character qualities do you want your child to have firmly in place by adulthood?

4. Can you envision the educational benefits of family life?

5. Are you prepared to make a long-term investment in your child? How do you see that playing out in your particular situation?

CHAPTER 7

Feeling Stuck

Overcoming Obstacles

One of the biggest and most common obstacles parents face in regard to homeschooling is fear: fear of not being enough, fear of failure, fear of adverse circumstances, fear of failing our kids, fear that our kids won't measure up, fear that we won't measure up, fear that our kids won't be "successful," and fear of what other people think.

We face these same fears in parenting, yet most of us chose to become parents anyway. And when we face challenges as parents, most of us don't choose to stop being parents. Instead, out of deep love, concern, and care for our kids, we press on, we become resourceful, and we figure it out.

The same is true when it comes to homeschooling. One of the first steps to overcoming our fears is to face them one at a time, and then move forward in spite of them. As time passes, we begin to see how those overwhelming challenges are actually opportunities. They are, in fact, calls to action.

The deep love God has placed in our hearts for our kids is the force that drives us to go to the ends of the earth for the good of our children. This means the things we fear most can be a source of motivation to do whatever it takes to secure the safety and well-being of our children—physically, mentally, emotionally, and spiritually.

This is why more and more families are choosing to homeschool. Instead of being afraid, they are often surprised to find themselves loving the freedom and flexibility, the broadened perspective on their children's potential and what education really looks like. It's liberating, it's organic, and it's beautiful in so many unexpected ways. But it requires us to look fear squarely in the eyes and stand in the gap to protect our children from what we believe may be harmful to them.

According to God's Word and his created order, our role as parents is God-given. This means we have authority to decide what is right for our children. We are facilitators of all things concerning them, which includes their education. When I decide to send my children to school, that means I am giving permission to everyone involved there—from the administrators to the teachers to the other students—to influence my children. I may think my children are in good hands, but the responsibility for whether or not that is true still falls directly on my shoulders as a parent.

Parents who decide to homeschool believe they can provide a better learning environment for their kids. It doesn't mean they don't have doubts or fears, and it certainly doesn't mean they won't have to overcome obstacles. However, they are willing to move forward in courage and hope because they see an opportunity for something better for their kids, and they're willing to do the work.

The fact that we are believers is significant. It means we

have direct access to the God who created our kids. The fact that he loves them even more than we do gives us a huge advantage. We don't have to be so concerned with where we don't feel qualified because our "inadequacies" are of *no* concern to God. They are *not* an obstacle to him! It's a truth I've seen play out over and over again in the lives of parents who choose to meet their fears head-on.

To give you inspiration and courage, I want to share several true stories from actual families who faced seemingly impossible obstacles when they decided to homeschool their kids. However, instead of shrinking in fear, they forged ahead for the sake of their children and found that God did above and beyond all they could ask or imagine. I asked each parent to share three things: the obstacle(s) they faced, how they moved forward, and what happened as a result. The stories that follow are told in their own words.

JENNY

Our son, Gideon, was nine when we adopted him. He has ASD (autism spectrum disorder), PTSD (post-traumatic stress disorder), FASD (fetal alcohol spectrum disorder), and ADHD (attention deficit hyperactivity disorder). While we worked on finalizing his adoption, he was enrolled in our local public school. When the adoption was finalized in April, we were strongly encouraged to let him finish out the year in public school. We were told his needs were too great for us, and he needed professional help due to his violent outbursts and angry behaviors. We were also told he was non-compliant in taking basic achievement tests to evaluate his academic strengths and struggles. We were told we could never give him the support he needs.

When Gideon's special needs teacher was fired, we were not informed. Nor were we told that they had been locking

Gideon in a de-escalation room for safety. We are pro-safety, but it's against state law not to inform the parents within twenty-four hours after this occurs. We only found out when it was mentioned during a parent-teacher conference. Every single time we visited him in his classroom, Gideon was miserable and screaming and throwing a tantrum. We felt he needed the stability and flexibility of a home education environment.

We conducted achievement testing the same month we removed Gideon from public school. The testing told us he was at a kindergarten to first-grade level. We found a curriculum that matched his learning style and wrote an SEP (Student Education Plan), which is the homeschool version of the public school IEP (Individualized Education Program). Gideon is now eleven years old and making steady progress. He's made up three grade levels in two years. We give him frequent breaks, flexibility, and the encouragement he needs. He's thriving!

FELICIA

Shelby, my oldest child, was born an achondroplastic dwarf and profoundly deaf. She is also missing most of her myelin sheath, an insulating membrane that forms around nerves in the brain and spinal cord.

When I initially sought help from local organizations and the school district, I was bombarded with several opinions from professionals, many of them contradictory. In our state, the public schools require special needs kids to attend school beginning at age three. Because my husband did not see homeschooling as an option, we tried regional day school for the deaf (services at home), a cluster site school (on site about forty-five minutes away), and a private deaf school forty-five minutes away. By the time Shelby was five, we decided it wasn't working and began our homeschool journey. We realized we knew our child best, and she needed a specific educational plan that the school district couldn't provide.

Shelby is now twenty-one. (We ended up having seven more children and homeschooling all of them as well.) Although she was homeschooled for most of her education, Shelby chose to also attend Texas School for the Deaf (TSD) because it was her dream to be a florist, and TSD was the fastest way to do that. She now has a certificate in floral design from Austin Community College!

JENA

Our homeschooling obstacle was a tornado that destroyed our home. We ended up living in three different locations as we searched for a new home. We also suffered health problems, enduring one illness after another. Trying to maintain homeschooling in the midst of all the upheaval was exhausting. We decided to hit the "pause" button and simply rest in the Lord for a while.

As best we could, we kept moving forward for the sake of our children because we did not want this time in their lives to cause permanent harm. They each had their own healing to do after the tornado, and they watched us deal with similar struggles. We tried to make the healing process as open and light as possible so it could be part of our kids' education. We took small steps forward and rested in the rhythms of simple days. Friends offered support and grace when we needed to take a break.

The results have been better than I could have expected. I worried at first how an extended break might impact our children, but by the end of that school year, there were no deficits. The Lord provided in every way possible. We rested, we healed from trauma and illness, we built new lives in a new home, and we are thriving. *Trust* and *obey* have been the ongoing themes of this season for our family.

BIANCA

We had some bad experiences with our three kids in the school system. For example, within a week of starting kindergarten, one of our daughter's classmates had been "pantsed" by a classmate. I was shocked. Our daughter came home tired every day and started using language we didn't approve of. Having attended public school myself, I was very aware of the kind of pressures a young girl experiences, and I wanted to protect our daughter from those as well.

Another factor was our son's leukemia diagnosis. The logistics of his treatment plan were intense, and we simply couldn't see how our family could navigate this journey while we were separated every day.

Most importantly, we couldn't see our kids growing in their faith by attending school. Nothing related to our life of faith would be encouraged or even allowed—no prayer, no hymns, no Jesus! I felt like I wouldn't be doing my job as a Christian mom by sending my kids to public school.

The results have been all for the better! There have been ups and downs, but at the end of the day, we have been together and the Lord guides each of our days. Our middle child has now started kindergarten and my children are protected from the negative influences of public school. We have gained a strong family identity!

SPRING

If you had asked me about homeschooling a few years ago, I would have said, "No way! That is not for me." I didn't think it was good for all the Christian families to be taken out of our public school. Christian children are the arrows that we shoot into the world. Although I still feel strongly that they are our arrows and we are sending them into the world, I've also come to believe that our children need time to build a solid foundation first.

Even though I was mentally closed off to the idea of homeschooling, I felt a little tug on my heart about it. God knows how stubborn I can be at times, and he had to force my hand a little. That happened when California passed a law prohibiting unvaccinated children from attending school. For various personal and medical reasons, we had decided not to do all the vaccinations, so we were forced to homeschool.

Having our seven kids home has allowed us to bond as a family. We are more tuned into the needs of our children and have the privilege of watching them grow by leaps and bounds. If our kids were still in public school, we would be missing far too much of that. We are learning to let God lead us and resisting the temptation to let curriculum rule our days. Having a more unhurried, peaceful approach has been the best thing for our family.

I never thought I would love homeschooling my kids so much! In spite of my doubts, I *am* doing it, and they are all learning. I'm realizing how time flies, so I need to take in all the moments I can and make them the best for our family. Sometimes I feel like a failure at this, but I'm learning to slow down and enjoy life so much more. I especially love the flexibility in our days—we can get up and go to a park, zoo, tide pools, or take a family field trip without having to get permission to be absent from school. There seems to be more peace and calm overall for our family and for me!

JENNI

My oldest child was struggling to learn even the basics when we first started kindergarten at home. My approach wasn't working with him and neither was the curriculum. We were both overwhelmed, and I doubted my ability to continue the journey in homeschooling.

My heart, however, knew it was the right thing to do. My husband also remembered the challenges he had in public school and felt it was crucial to move forward with home-schooling.

Because homeschooling wasn't initially on my radar, I knew it was a God thing. I also couldn't imagine giving up—I knew my child better than anyone else, and I would fight harder for him than anyone. I wanted to discover how to best support my son's learning, and I knew it would take time. Having a struggling learner didn't change my desire; it simply changed my approach.

When we became unhurried homeschoolers, I was able to take the time to become a student of my child's learning style. That's when we discovered he is dyslexic and designed his learning around the gifts he's been blessed with. Four years later, we have a boy who laughs with enjoyment during lessons, reads fluently, and has developed a level of perseverance I admire. I'm so grateful that our family has grown closer in ways that only spending time together at home every day allows.

ASHLEY

When we decided to homeschool, we had five kids ages six and under. With so many littles at home, I felt I would not be able to provide my kids with the education they deserved. Honestly, God had to nudge me pretty firmly.

I have a best friend who is passionate about homeschooling. She planted seeds in my heart for years. Shortly after my daughter completed kindergarten in public school, our family doctor even suggested I homeschool! I felt like it *had* to be a God nudge, so I opened my mind a bit more. Then I watched a video on Facebook about the importance of taking our children's spiritual well-being into our own hands by homeschooling. That sealed the deal for me. I didn't want to rely on anyone else to teach my children how to behave or what to believe, especially about matters of faith. So I felt very strongly that if God was calling me to do this, he would provide the way—and he has!

Almost every day of this past homeschooling year, my heart has been filled with gratitude that I am able to watch my daughter grow more than I could if she was gone for seven hours a day, five days a week. I hadn't recognized it at the time, but during her kindergarten year, I felt jealous of her teacher because she got to watch her learn and grow during the day, while I had to deal with the tired daughter who was cranky at the end of the day. I also had to try to keep up with her homework, then rush her to bed in order to be sure she could get out the door bright and early the next morning.

I have been "unschooling" her this year by encouraging her to stay a child for a little longer and explore her world according to her passions. We have enjoyed playing in a creek, swimming, and horseback riding. We have visited aquariums, tree farms, and parks. We've had play dates, gone to music class, put puzzles together, and spent extended time in nature. It's been such an enriching year!

I feel strongly that she is a brighter young girl because we are giving her the time and space she needs to grow emotionally and spiritually before we even think about filling her mind with academics.

TERESA

When I began homeschooling, my biggest obstacle was understanding the difference between "schooling at home" and "homeschooling." Schooling at home is basically implementing the public school approach to education in a home setting. We schooled at home for a couple of years, and it squashed my daughter's love of learning. In contrast, homeschooling is about having the freedom to choose the program and approach that's best for your child.

Even though those first couple of years were hard, I moved forward out of a strong belief that homeschooling is what we are supposed to do. Although I don't believe homeschooling is holier than other educational choices, I do believe it is God's will for my family—and the results have been astounding! When I learned to homeschool my daughter rather than school her at home—using a mixture of homeschooling and unschooling—things got so much better.

She is now a high school senior and has already been working for two years in her chosen field. She will have a large portion of her certification completed before graduation, and her entrepreneur business is totally set up. Taking her out of public school in fourth grade was the best move I ever made, and I'm so thankful we pushed through the hard years.

My son is entering third grade and loves to learn. Homeschooling has been a perfect fit for him. We did interest-led learning for the first two years but are now choosing a more structured approach. He excels in some subjects and is slower in others, but he's working at his own pace and learning so much.

KELLI

I decided to begin homeschooling when my kids were heading into seventh, sixth, fifth (twins), and third grades. At that time, I was married. Four years later, I found myself separated without any financial help from my husband. He never came back, and we were divorced in 2018.

The obstacle I faced even before the divorce was how I

would be able to juggle working and homeschooling. After the divorce, it quickly transitioned into how I would provide for my kids while homeschooling.

Not homeschooling was not an option I would allow myself to entertain. I prayed and trusted God to help me. And he did, in every way I needed!

I became a childcare provider (non-licensed) and currently care for three little ones. I have never been in a place where I've made a lot of money, but I've always been able to pay the bills.

God has always provided what I needed for curriculum, whether it was through someone lending me theirs, finding books for free or inexpensively at a local used bookstore, or God providing the money for new ones. We have always had what we needed.

This journey of homeschooling has grown my faith and trust in God. I cling to his Word and know that he will equip me with what I need to accomplish his will.

DEBBIE

We have a son with autism and a daughter with dyslexia. After homeschooling for five years, I miscarried at sixteen weeks. I kept asking myself how I could trust God and continue homeschooling while delivering and holding my baby in the palm of my hand, healing from the emotional trauma and spiraling toward depression and anxiety.

I decided to move forward anyway, based on the knowledge that my husband and children still needed me and that God's purpose in my life was not finished. The Holy Spirit spoke straight to my heart in the darkest moments when my thoughts felt like poison.

Now, my autistic son has moved into upper middle school and my dyslexic daughter is reading everything she can get her hands on!

I get to see my husband's business prosper and my children share their faith and grow in their understanding of God's Word. This has been the hardest season of my life, but I continue to hold onto his hand, which covers me always.

Even in a season of difficulty, by God's grace, we are moving forward with our homeschool adventures!

These are just a few of the many stories I have heard from parents who decided to move forward with courage in spite of their doubts and concerns. They trusted that somehow, in spite of the obstacles, they would ultimately find the educational path that was best for their children. When they did, there was no turning back!

REAL-LIFE APPLICATION

1. What are your three greatest fears when it comes to home education?

2. Which of the stories in this chapter can you most relate to?

3. In which of the stories did you find the most inspiration?

CHAPTER 8

Reverse Engineering Your Kids' Education

Someone once said, "Be stubborn about your goals, but flexible about your methods."

Nothing could be truer when it comes to homeschooling.

With that in mind, I have a confession to make: *I have never used a lesson planner.*

It wasn't that I didn't have some sort of daily plan for our children, but I learned early on, after briefly trying to lesson plan the conventional way, that it was an exercise in futility for me.

To start with, if I wrote the plan, I felt like I had to make sure the plan happened, or I was a failure as a homeschool mom. For me, plans quickly become expectations. The sooner I admitted that and made an adjustment, the better.

From very early on, I saw that if I wanted my kids to love learning, most of the time I had to let them determine the direction. Because I had no way of knowing at any given hour, day, week, month, or year what my kids' interests might be, I found it both stressful and counterproductive to do much planning. I couldn't see into the future and know that dinosaurs would be a thing for one child for three months and baking would be of interest to another for an afternoon. I also couldn't predict what they would ultimately learn from those interests.

So instead of writing detailed plans, I wrote skeleton plans that allowed for flexibility.

I wasn't comfortable having no plan at all, but instead of having an all-or-nothing mentality, I decided to keep a looser grip by keeping my plan simple. I made sure math, reading, and writing happened each day, but the rest of the time, I focused on teaching through family life and allowing a good chunk of free time in the afternoons.

Today, one might even call my approach "innovative." The definition of innovation is, "The practical translation of ideas into new or improved products, services, processes, systems or social interactions." Because my only experience when it came to education was with a traditional classroom setting, I had to take an innovative approach to that system, using the parts that worked for our family and eliminating or reinventing the parts that didn't.

Three Basic Goals

Ultimately, my husband and I had three basic goals when it came to our kids' education:

- To grow *lifelong learners*.
- To grow kids who were *resourceful*.
- To grow kids who had a *strong work ethic*.

We strongly believed that if our kids embraced these attributes, they would be successful at whatever they were called to do. But in order to be sure that we were consistently moving toward these goals, we needed to begin each day with the end in mind. Essentially, that meant we needed to reverse engineer our kids' education—to determine our learning outcomes first and then create the curriculum or lessons to achieve those outcomes.

Lifelong Learners

To grow into lifelong learners it was essential that our kids knew basic math and how to read and write.

To encourage our kids to become lifelong learners, learning needed to be primarily enjoyable, and it was always best if they learned by engaging something in which they had an interest. That meant we had to give them time to follow their curiosities, and as they did, we watched for those interests that would become deeper pursuits.

Resourceful

If they were going to be resourceful, we had to challenge them to figure things out on their own, to be problem solvers. When they ran into obstacles, we tried not to give them answers immediately, but instead asked questions that encouraged them to solve the problems they faced. This could apply to their relationships with their siblings, a math problem, chores, hobbies, or a myriad of other life circumstances.

Strong Work Ethic

Developing a strong work ethic meant we gave them chores, inspected their chores, encouraged them, and showed them how to do new things. Someone once said, "Don't expect what you're not willing to *inspect*."

All of this takes time, so it only made sense that there needed to be plenty of margin in our days, hence the skeleton schedule.

Productive Play

We did have an important caveat for the kids' independent (self-directed?) time: it had to be productive. To us, productive play could look like a lot of things: creating something with their hands, their heads, or their hearts. It could look like anything from building a fort, drawing, baking (something tangible) to observing nature or simply watching the clouds and daydreaming. All of these activities produce something, even if it's simply expanding the imagination. The idea of encouraging productivity was based on the principle that we wanted to raise adults who were producers, not just consumers. Being a consumer is a passive role. It doesn't take a lot of creativity or innovation to be a consumer, and it doesn't really make the world a better place. Encouraging our kids to be productive during their free time helped move them toward our ultimate goals for them: becoming lifelong learners, being resourceful, and building a strong work ethic. It also inspired innovation.

Encourage Innovation

When a child comes up with a way to build a better bike jump, negotiates to get a toy his brother is playing with, or creates a recipe with limited ingredients, he or she is practicing innovation.

Children are not typically innovative when they are bogged down with too much bookwork, an overcrowded schedule, or too much busy work that seems irrelevant to them. In order to encourage innovation, kids need time and space for creativity to flow freely in an environment that leaves open as many options as possible. In other words, they need an environment that *does* encourage exploration and that *doesn't* insist on a results-driven outcome.

Again, this is the beauty of homeschooling. We have control over the environment in which our children are immersed. We can naturally offer them multiple areas to explore as they move through their days. We share our lives with our kids, inviting them into the things we are already doing (cooking, hobbies, grocery shopping, etc.), and letting them take initiative if they are interested or giving them freedom to explore on their own.

For example, if we were building a birdhouse, we might bring the kids outside with us. We might show them what we are doing, inviting them to watch if they want to. We might also set out the tools, nails, and wood to investigate. If they seem uninterested, we may or may not make a suggestion or two, but ultimately, we let them decide what they want to do with what they have been offered, even if that means they walk away and do something else. Whether our kids stay with us through the project or choose something else, we keep an open mind, always asking, "Where could this possibly lead?"

Instead of making decisions that continually narrow the options, we loosen our grip on what we think our kids should be learning and let learning happen more naturally, offering as many options for as long as possible.

Often, this requires allowing our kids to be bored.

Let Them Confront Boredom

I mentioned always encouraging productivity, even during free time but sometimes our kids are most productive and creative as a result of feeling like there's nothing to do. It's from that place of boredom that the creative juices can begin to flow.

One of the questions many new homeschooling parents ask is, "How do I keep my kids busy all day?" If you are not used to having your kids home that much, it can certainly feel intimidating. You may be envisioning the days of summer break when the kids are constantly saying they're bored, and you feel like you're going to lose your mind. Allow me to let you in on a little secret: *It's not your job to entertain your kids all day.* In fact, it's essential that you *don't* entertain them all day.

Our kids learned quickly to never use the word "bored," because that meant they would immediately be assigned a chore. In fact, I kept a list of chores handy to ward off complaining, disrespect, and aimlessness. I also followed my mom's example and had a jar with little slips of paper in it. Written on each slip was either a fun activity or a chore. If our kids said they were bored, they had to take a slip of paper from the jar, and it was a toss-up what they would end up having to do. It wasn't that I didn't want to hear the word "bored," but rather, I wanted our kids to be able to find their own direction and self-entertain without depending on me for all of their ideas.

A Relaxed Rhythm Pays Off

Because our mornings always started with directed productivity (chores and schoolwork), I believe that set the tone for the rest of the day. If our days had started with little to no direction, I suspect complaints of boredom might have been more of a problem.

Our adult kids have told me that one of the things they loved most about homeschooling was the fact that they felt like they were getting their "work" or "have-tos" done in the mornings, because this taught them to do the hard things first. They were also much more motivated to get their schoolwork done in the mornings, knowing that if they did, they would have free time in the afternoons. This simple schedule established a relaxed rhythm to our days, but I still sometimes wondered if it was enough. I had no way of knowing for sure if it really would be, so it was a faith walk, but God encouraged me along the way. Eventually, God gave me even more confirmation at just the right time.

Our kids were involved in a homeschool program where they attended extracurricular classes one day a week. In order to attend, I was required to write a monthly progress report on what they were learning at home. I'll admit I was intimidated at first. I was concerned that our more relaxed approach would not translate well on paper, and I would have to sacrifice what seemed to be working for us in order to meet more requirements.

As time passed, I actually began to appreciate those monthly reports more and more. As I thought back over each month and wrote out even a fraction of what we did, I realized how much learning was happening. It was amazing! Instead of making me feel inadequate, the short reports helped me relax and enjoy homeschooling even more. The evidence was clear: my kids *were* learning in a fraction of the time it would likely have taken in a traditional classroom setting. On top of that, they were enjoying it, and our family was making memories that would last a lifetime!

If you feel uncomfortable with the approach our family took, that's OK! It's important to remember that each family is different and has to make its own way in the homeschooling journey. You can glean from my story whatever resonates with your heart for your kids. The important thing to remember is that you *can* find your way one step at a time. Be patient with yourself. Learn to trust the heart God has given you for your kids and, most importantly, listen to God's heart for your family.

Even if you were not allowed to be innovative in your own education and wonder what that might look like for your family, I can promise you this: *As long as you continue to learn how to learn alongside your kids, you will be thrilled with the results!*

Remember, kids are curious by nature, and learning comes quite naturally for them, especially when we don't insist on a results-driven outcome but leave room for as many learning options for as long as possible. Be a student of your kids. Watch where learning is happening, and encourage it in all forms.

If you are concerned about whether or not your kids are learning enough, consider keeping a daily journal. Write down when you see your child engaged in learning whether that is taking something apart and putting it back together, exploring outside, or baking cookies alongside you. For example: "Ella (four years old) carefully measured ingredients into the bowl. We talked about how fractions are part of a whole measurement. While pouring the ingredients in, keeping the bowl stable, and stirring, she practiced hand/eye coordination and spatial awareness. She learned the difference between 'stirring' and 'folding' and practiced following verbal directions."

Another example would be something like this: "Nate looked at a book on dinosaurs, carefully examining each page and noticing how the dinosaurs were alike and how they were different. He used play dough to try to replicate them. He used communication skills to explain what he observed along with spatial awareness, and fine motor skills."

You can write in your journal throughout the day or wait and do it at the end of the day. I am confident that as you do this, you will become more aware of all that your kids really *are* learning. As a result, you will find more specific direction for your family, and you will grow in confidence that homeschooling is, in fact, a great educational choice.

Be Willing to Make Changes

When he was fifteen, our son, Silas, struggled with math. I felt like he was capable of learning the concepts, but the math curriculum that had worked well for the previous couple of years wasn't working well anymore. The level he was working at was already beyond me, so I couldn't really help him.

I prayed about it and waited. One day, I happened to talk with a friend who mentioned (with no prompting from me) that she was loving the simplicity of a certain math program she was using with her kids. I'm all about simplicity, as it has often proven beneficial for our kids. So I had Silas take the placement test for this other program, which would tell me which grade level he should be working at. The results? *Fifth grade*. My heart sank just a bit. I truly thought he would place at a higher grade level because he was working at grade level in the other curriculum.

I reminded myself of my goals: I wanted to raise a lifelong learner. If Silas continued to be frustrated with math, he would begin to believe he was a math failure, and no amount of telling him otherwise would change his mind. He needed math he could do mostly on his own, but which also progressively challenged him. If his challenges weren't overwhelming, he would be able to overcome them (as a problem solver) and he would continue to persevere (with a strong work ethic).

I also knew that if Silas had a weakness somewhere in his basic math skills, this would be a good time to firm up those skills before starting high school. So even though I cringed a bit, I ordered the fifth-grade math unit.

Fortunately, Silas made his way through workbook after workbook with little to no trouble and actually enjoyed it. Although he hadn't finished the fifth-grade curriculum by the end of the school year, we decided to go ahead and do his end-of-year testing. I almost fell over when I read the results. His math scores were at a college freshman level!

I had never hung my hat on test results, but now I knew that, at the very least, Silas was ready for high school, and whatever gaps he might still have weren't significant. We had met the goal of making sure he was solid in the basics. I could relax and move forward with confidence.

This was a clear reminder of how important it is to keep the end in mind, and not to limit the paths we can take to get there. It helps to think of the journey as a winding path rather than a straight one. That might be a bit unsettling if you are a planner like me, but as I've walked out taking a more unhurried approach with our kids, I have been reminded over and over again that God has a far better plan than I could ever create on my own. He doesn't want us to feel continually stressed and burdened over our kids' education, so he purposely made them curious by nature and adept at learning a great deal on their own.

You definitely have an important part in the education process, but maybe not in all the ways you once thought you would. The key is to keep your hands and heart open, and keep learning how to learn alongside your kids!

1. If you could write a short mission statement (call it a rough draft for now), what would it say?

2. Do you believe that independent (self-directed) time is an important part of your kids' day? Why?

3. If you could envision a more relaxed rhythm to your homeschool days, what might that look like?

CHAPTER 9

In the Beginning
Babies and Toddlers

As a parent, chances are you began to feel pressure from the moment you found out you were expecting. And by pressure, I mean the weight of other people's opinions and advice. You were given countless opinions about how to feed, clothe, and even educate your child. Maybe you felt pressure to decide on your parenting style before your child was even born. Feeling pushed and pressured is no way to start your parenting journey, so it's important early on to grow in parental discernment.

Developing Parental Discernment

Parental discernment is being able to identify what's best for you and your child, regardless of anyone else's opinion. To grow in parental discernment is to develop sharp perceptions and good judgments tuning into *our* kids. For Christians, discernment also means "determining God's desire in a situation [or for one's life as a whole] . . . or identifying the true nature of a thing [whether or not it is good]."[1]

We need parental discernment because the pressures of parenting will never go away. In fact, they only intensify as your child gets older. There will always be someone—or many someones—who has opinions about what's best for your child. Doing the work to find your footing as a parent is time well spent, and you'll save yourself a lot of grief by doing it sooner rather than later. In other words, the need for parental discernment starts from the moment you discover you're going to be a parent.

Having parental discernment does not mean we should never take advice, counsel, or correction, but it does require being prepared when well-meaning people insert their strong opinions into our lives whether we want them to or not. I've walked away from more than one conversation wondering what just happened. I was a ball of emotions and felt like a failure, and I wasn't sure why.

When one of our sons was a toddler, he was what might be referred to as a "spitfire." Even at one and two years old, he had a very strong sense of justice. If he felt he'd been wronged, he became obstinate, angry, and vocal about it. Or, when things didn't go his way, he threw a tantrum. Darryl and I had a good handle on him, or at least I thought so, until a well-meaning person in our lives, whom I respected, said otherwise. This person essentially told us that we were being poor parents, that our son was headed in a bad direction, and we needed to clamp down on him.

I took this advice to heart, even though I'd already been a parent for several years and something about it felt off. I tried "clamping down" on my son in the suggested ways and almost immediately had a strong feeling of aversion in my gut. I could also see the life being sucked out of our son, and I simply couldn't take it.

When Darryl and I talked about it, he had the perfect response: "Durenda, God has given our son to *us* to raise," he said, "so God is not going to give the wisdom we need to parent our son to someone else. He's going to give it to *us*."

Trusting God for the parenting wisdom we need doesn't mean God won't sometimes use other people in our lives to mentor us in our parenting journey. But at the end of the day, it is we, the parents, who are ultimately responsible for all things concerning our kids—how they are raised, educated, and cared for. This is why it's crucial that we begin to develop parental discernment from day one.

In case you're wondering how the story of our son played out, his strong sense of justice has led him to be a man of integrity and a defender of what is true and right. He has been a continual blessing to us and others. Where he is concerned, I can tell you that God has been faithful. In fact, in the midst of that experience, God brought me to a Scripture that confirmed the direction Darryl and I had decided to take:

> Trust in the LORD and do good.
>> Then you will live safely in the land and prosper.
> Take delight in the LORD,
>> and he will give you your heart's desires.
>
> Commit everything you do to the LORD.
>> Trust him, and he will help you.
> He will make your innocence radiate like the dawn,
>> and the justice of your cause will shine like the
>> noonday sun. (Ps. 37:3–6)

It was as though God was saying that time would prove whether we were doing right by our son. We simply had to be patient and walk in trusting obedience toward what God was directing us to do.

Pressures and challenges are to be expected all along the path of our parenting journeys. We are never going to have everyone's approval. It's an exercise in futility even to try. Our time and energy are far better spent focusing on what God has entrusted to us and doing what he is asking us to do.

I often envision this process as tending our backyard. We are responsible to tend our own backyards, not someone else's. It can be easy to look over the fence and criticize our neighbor's backyard—or for our neighbor to criticize our backyard—but again, our time is better spent working in our own backyard. Goodness knows there's always plenty to do!

Children Are God's Blessing

The challenges of parenting are faith building, for sure. That's why it's so important to remember that God calls children a blessing, a gift, a heritage (see Psalm 127:3). It's sometimes difficult to feel that way when we are sleep deprived or they are trying our patience for the hundredth time. But that doesn't make what God says about them untrue.

When Darryl and I married, he wanted two children. I didn't tell him I wanted ten. I knew he was the man for me, and I was confident that God could deal with the difference in our numbers by changing either his heart or mine. And he did.

After our third child was born, we were a family of two girls and one boy. Darryl thought that was plenty, but my heart was aching at the thought of not considering more children. I prayed and prayed and prayed some more. I read many good books by others who believed children were a blessing. I read excerpts to my husband, but I also tried not to make it obvious how much I didn't want to be done having kids.

Eventually, he looked at me and said, "There are lots of opinions on having kids or not having kids, but I think the only one that really matters is God's. So I'm going to locate every verse in the Bible that talks about kids, and see what I find."

After doing his research, he announced, "Well, I can't find a single verse in the Bible that has anything negative to say about kids. In fact, the opposite is true. Every time I turn around, I read verses that say that they are a blessing, a reward, and a *really* good thing. So if God says they are good and a blessing, why would I want to limit how many he gives us?"

The rest is history.

To be clear, I am not saying every Christian couple should have as many kids as possible. I am saying to approach that decision prayerfully and with the biblical mindset that children are truly a blessing. Then, let God lead you in this part of your life as much as any other.

As Darryl and I lived out this mindset, God added more children to our family (in spite of several miscarriages), and our faith deepened as we trusted God for provision financially, emotionally, mentally, spiritually, and physically. Yes, we faced challenges we might not have faced if we'd had fewer children, but as we framed our thinking around the promise that children are a blessing, we realized that every trial and hardship brought us closer to each other and grew our faith.

When I got frustrated as a mom or felt like the kids were driving me crazy, I asked God to show me how they were a blessing in that particular situation. Sometimes I discovered how much I needed God (which is always a good thing), or realized he was leading us in a different and better direction in our schooling, lifestyle, or any number of other areas. God used the kids to refine our family's lifestyle.

Thirty years later, I can tell you that there isn't one kid I would send back—every one of them truly is a blessing. But during those years of growing and raising our family, there were countless people who made comments about our life choices. Many were good, but some were not. We experienced deeply hurtful moments when others spouted unsolicited opinions. We quickly learned that many people don't see kids as a blessing and have no respect for children.

None of our children are deaf, so they sometimes heard the snide comments and watched our response. We were always kind to the naysayers but made it clear that we thought kids were awesome, especially ours. Often, we talked about those comments with our kids afterward to be sure they knew how happy we were that they were part of our family and to explain that sometimes, other people simply didn't get it. It was almost like we had a great little secret we were thoroughly enjoying—that kids are awesome—and those who didn't understand were simply missing out on all the fun!

Because our kids were well behaved, I can honestly say that most of the time, people's comments were positive. However, when people first found out we homeschooled, that could open another can of worms. After a while, we became somewhat impervious to any negativity. Once we decided that we were doing what was best for *our* family, we quickly developed the conviction that we had better things to do than worry about what people thought.

The funny thing is, through that process, our kids

learned to do the same. They are independent thinkers and do not have a herd mentality. They are team players and care deeply for others, but they also know what makes a good team, and that's where they want to be.

As you add children to your family, know that they are all a blessing.

Sibling Relationships and Home Education

When you are homeschooling multiple ages, it can feel like you aren't getting as much bookwork done as you would like, but when you change your thinking to include sibling relationships—including the care of babies and toddlers—as an important part of your kids' education, it's a game changer.

When our kids were early elementary-age and younger, I tried to do our school activities in twenty-minute increments. For example, while doing reading lessons with one child, I had another care for the baby and another play with the toddler. I had certain games, puzzles, or activities they could do *only* during "sibling time" to keep it special. Sometimes I let the older child choose the play dough, books, games, or supplies for their special time with their younger sibling.

As the kids got a little older, our oldest child, who by then was reading well and could follow directions, did reading lessons with the beginning reader. This made her feel very grown up. She enjoyed it so much, she taught every upcoming reader after that. I taught the first three of our eight kids to read, then she taught the rest (except for our youngest, who had some learning struggles, but that's another story).

No matter where you are in growing your family, homeschooling is not only doable but also beneficial in teaching life skills to our kids. When we embrace the fact that family life is an optimal place to give our kids a full education, we are suddenly able to see the opportunities in front of us to raise healthy and productive adults!

I often have moms with young children reach out to me because they feel like they're failing at educating their older kids. For instance, one mom told me she felt she was not handling homeschooling well because her second-grade son couldn't write a report.

First of all, if you know anything about boys, especially young boys, they are not typically developmentally ready for report writing by second grade. What they *are* ready for is lots of physical activity: catching frogs, building forts, riding bikes, digging in the dirt, and maybe some reading out loud along with simple math and copy work.

All that to say, you can relax. Don't miss out on enjoying your children—your blessings—because of unrealistic expectations. A little bit of schoolwork that is enjoyable, rather than copious amounts that end up feeling tedious, will move your child much farther along in their education by encouraging a love of learning.

Moms and dads, we are life-givers, nurturers, and encouragers. Enjoy that process, whether it is with your babies, toddlers, or older children. Homeschool from the heart that God has given you. In other words, let the nurturing nature that comes naturally guide you. It may feel like not enough or it may feel awkward to start with, but eventually, you'll find your rhythm. Be your kids' greatest fans and biggest encouragers, and you will be surprised how much they learn on their own.

Have you ever noticed that you don't have to take your toddler to a class to teach them to talk? First of all, they learn the most simply by being around people who talk. You may encourage them by repeating words, watching their responses, or cheering them on when they say something new. This isn't much different from other types of learning. Kids are so much smarter than we give them credit for.

Again, this goes back to developing a respect for children, which in turn grows out of believing they are a blessing. The world is lacking in this perspective. When we give our kids the time and space to develop naturally, on their own, it opens up a vast array of possibilities. As we see these possibilities unfold, we become more confident and less stressed about our perceived inadequacies as parents. When that shift happens, we have grown in parental discernment.

It starts from the beginning by fully embracing the fact that children are a blessing, by respecting their developmental stages, and by understanding that God is the one who knits our families together through his ways and in his timing.

In his eyes, no baby is ill-timed.

From the day your child is born, the goal is to spend time getting to know them, becoming an expert in *your* child. During the early years, learn as much as you can about your child, about yourself, and about your family tendencies. Find out what brings life to your family, what works and what doesn't. Understand that some things may be conducive to one season and not another, but the point is to know when something is working and when it isn't. This is all part of developing parental discernment and will help prepare you for the years ahead.

Our oldest two daughters are now married with children of their own. Although they are just twenty-one months apart in age, they are very different personalities. One is more scheduled and the other is not as much. One chose more of an attachment style of early parenting and the other not so much. They both breastfed their babies, but one chose more of a demand-based feeding schedule and the other did not. It was a delight to see each one doing what worked well for her and what resonated with her heart as a mom. They both knew they had the freedom to make those choices and began to develop their parental discernment early. Do they ever doubt themselves? Of course; every parent does. But ultimately, they continue to challenge themselves to trust in God's heart and direction for their family.

God has good plans for us and our families. Our job is to tend our own backyard by seeking his heart for *our* family. As we do, our unique family culture begins to unfold, and that's when the adventure begins!

YOU KNOW YOU ARE DEVELOPING PARENTAL DISCERNMENT WHEN:

- You don't think twice about what other people think. You can simply smile and nod when someone gives you unsolicited advice instead of feeling the need to defend your decisions.
- You decide it's not as important to be understood by others as it is to be inwardly at peace with your decisions.
- You realize your children don't need to be perfect. This means you choose to recognize the difference between childishness and foolishness. You decide it's OK for your kids to be kids while acknowledging that the journey toward wisdom is a process that happens slowly over time with your gentle encouragement.

- You recognize that your children were intentionally knit together by God with their own unique characteristics and purpose. This means you avoid comparing them to other children and continue to pray and watch for God's customized plan to unfold.

REAL-LIFE APPLICATION

1. In what ways do you feel like you need to grow more in parental discernment?

2. Do you ever find yourself changing how you respond to your children based on what someone else might say or think?

3. Have you fully embraced the truth that children are, in fact, a blessing from God? How might that affect how you live everyday life with your kids or how you view homeschooling?

4. Can you see the educational benefits of sibling relationships?

CHAPTER 10

Nurturing Seedlings
The Early School Years

At the tender age of four, when I was just one week into kindergarten, I found myself sitting in the principal's office with my teacher and my mom. I don't remember much about the conversation, just a feeling of relief when they all agreed I wasn't ready for school.

It wasn't that I was acting out, and I can honestly say I don't remember feeling upset or afraid at school. I do remember that more than once, I ended up in the nurse's office with a slight fever and not "looking well."

My mom and teacher were wise enough to realize I wasn't really sick, and I didn't have emotional, behavioral, or learning issues. I simply needed to be with my mom. I needed more time for my little mind and body to develop in the safety and security of home.

It's not surprising that a young child might find the transition to school difficult, but it's often just as difficult for parents. I can't even count how many moms have told me they cried when they sent their child off to school or cried even at the thought of sending them. Some were excited about their kids starting school, but once the newness wore off, they missed them terribly. I am convinced there is a legitimate reason for these reactions.

God placed in us a deep love and concern for our kids that even the best teachers and classmates can't match. We have been nurturing and teaching our children from day one. It only makes sense that being abruptly separated for several hours a day would be difficult. We want the best education for our kids, so we send them to school. But who decided that when our child is four or five years old, we are suddenly incapable of providing the best education? Here's how I put it in my book, *The Unhurried Homeschooler*:

> We taught our children how to sit up, walk, talk, and eat with utensils—so why do we freak out when it's time for them to learn to read?
>
> I think part of the problem is that we have too many voices trying to tell us too many things. This creates doubt in our hearts that we are capable of teaching our children—when it's much more likely we are the best teachers possible for our children.[1]

As the people who care for our kids more deeply than anyone, we can offer the environment that is most conducive to nurturing a love for learning simply because being an effective teacher is not about knowing all the information; it's about *knowing our children*. When we know our kids, we can more effectively and efficiently educate them—and that starts by simply giving them a warm, loving, engaged family life.

Early Years Needs

During the early school years (kindergarten through third grade), kids have a deep need for security. This need is best met by keeping a consistent and simple daily routine. They need us to bring a certain amount of order to their world, and when that doesn't happen, it often results in negative behavior.

When our kids are acting out, it's typically because they need something: comfort, counsel, or relief. They may not realize they are hungry, thirsty, or tired. It's our job to be cued in and help them get to the bottom of what their needs are, whether those are physical, mental, emotional, or spiritual. Maintaining a simple routine with regular times for sleeping, eating, working, and playing reduces the frequency of meltdowns and gives our kids security. They are much more at peace because they have confidence that their basic needs will be met in a timely manner. They don't have to be concerned about being in survival mode. When they have confidence their needs will be met, they are free to be kids. They can focus their time and energy on connecting with the world around them and, as a result, learning comes much more naturally.

At the same time their basic needs are being consistently met, we also want to gently move our kids toward age-appropriate independence. We do this by encouraging them to do things for themselves. We encourage them to make their own beds, tidy their rooms, help set the table, help unload the dishwasher, brush their teeth, pick up their toys, get a diaper and wipes when Mom is changing the baby, help carry in groceries, and more. We let them work alongside us as much as possible, showing them how to do things and letting them try.

I will warn you that this approach takes time. It's faster and easier to do things ourselves, but we have to keep the big picture in mind. Essentially, we are slowly training our kids to have an independent mindset, one that encourages them to try to overcome problems themselves before asking for help.

As we encourage our kids to do things for themselves, we also invite them into many of our everyday tasks as parents. Participating in our daily activities helps them begin to see themselves as an important part of the family as well as a part of the world around them. They get an early taste for what it feels like to be part of something bigger than themselves. *Every* activity has the potential to be educational. Coupled with the fact that kids at this age learn best by doing, they are inevitably learning far more than we realize.

When they match socks, they are finding "like" things. When they pretend to fold laundry, they are practicing hand-eye coordination and following directions. When we take them to the grocery store and have conversations about what we are shopping for, we help them develop pre-language skills through explanation and use of words that are new to them (vocabulary). When we let them take something from the shelf and put it in the cart, they are following directions and practicing both hand-eye coordination and spatial awareness. When we teach them how to respond appropriately to the cashier, we are teaching manners, communication, social skills, and respect. The older they get, the more we can explain, and the more skilled they become.

As we engage daily life with our kids alongside us, they become more confident and more independent. This naturally spills over into any bookwork they start doing as they move into the school years, which makes a world of difference in the amount of time and energy that is required of us. Don't get me wrong; home educating our kids does require time and energy, but it is far less overwhelming when we nurture a certain amount of confidence and independence.

Every parent deals with doubts about whether or not they will be able to tell when their kids are ready for something but, as I've already said, you don't have to have a degree to do this. You just need to be tuned into your child.

By the time your child is school age, you have already had numerous experiences that told you when they were moving toward a new milestone. You may have noticed little indicators and naturally began to encourage your child to start to practice a new skill such as sitting, crawling, or walking. You stayed close by, letting them make attempts and giving them just enough encouragement to stay motivated to keep trying. You also knew when it was time to stop working on that new skill based on your child's response. This is a perfect example of assessing readiness and nurturing growth in our children. We can take this same approach and apply it throughout the toddler, preschool, and early elementary years. Again, it simply requires that we be tuned in to our children, and the easiest way to be tuned in is to simply be with them. When young children spend the bulk of their day in the care of warm, loving, engaged parents, they quickly grow in confidence and healthy independence.

As I mentioned earlier, a healthy family life filled with simple daily activities is a perfect setting for our young children to thrive and for us to recognize opportunities to encourage learning. As we tune in to our kids and pay attention to ourselves in that process as well, we can keep them moving toward increasing independence.

I will tell you, though, that none of this goes well when we try to do too much in a day or are distracted. I cannot tell you how many times I have had to lay down my perfectionistic tendencies so I could slow down to the pace my child needed. If we are going to encourage independence and learning at opportune times, we will need to slow our pace over and over again in order to match the pace of our child.

Throughout our simple days, we include our little ones in our activities as much as we can, especially when they show an interest in something. The same is true when it comes to what most would call "schoolwork."

Learning in the Early Years

I never forced my kids to start learning to read. Instead, I read to them. I made sure there were always good books conveniently lying around, and they picked up the ones that interested them. They looked at the pictures or asked me to read to them. Sometimes, they got impatient when it took me too long to turn a page. That was my cue to ask them if they wanted to learn to read so they didn't have to wait for me. They usually said yes, and that's when we began simple, short reading lessons.

Kids are natural learners. When they feel the need to learn to read, they can cover a lot of ground very quickly. In fact, when we had older kids who were already reading, the younger ones simply wanted to keep up and were eager to read much sooner than their older siblings had been at the same age.

I never pushed past the point where they seemed done for the day, which was usually no more than twenty minutes. I wanted to leave a good taste in their mouths for reading lessons. Sometimes, when they were having a bad day and the lesson went south really fast, I had to resist the urge to push through. Instead, I would cut the child loose to play or do something else. I had to trust the process.

There is an ebb and flow to life, and there is an ebb and flow to learning, especially in the early years. The sooner we realize that an ebb won't be the demise of our kids' future, the better! In order to better understand the reasons for this ebb and flow to learning in the early years, there are several important things to keep in mind:

- There are developmental differences between boys and girls. Boys are typically six to twelve months less mature than girls at this age, which means it may take them longer to learn some skills. (Don't worry; they will catch up!)
- Children this age are more interested in the process than the outcome. For example, when baking cookies, a child may show interest in adding the ingredients and stirring (the process), but lose interest when it comes time to bake them (the outcome).
- Their eyes can be easily strained if they do too much close-up work. They need to be outside regularly, where they can focus at objects in the distance, in order for their eyes to develop properly.
- They struggle to sit still because they are made to move at this age. They need to be exploring, running, playing, and letting off energy!
- They steadily improve at receiving correction because they are getting better at reasoning things out. We can utilize this to teach them self-control.

- They quickly forget things and are easily distracted, but our gentle and timely reminders help this part of their brain develop.
- They are beginning to develop a conscience. Their moral code is being established, and we get to help with that formation. This is one of the many benefits of both homeschooling and of taking an unhurried approach.
- Their large muscles are more developed than their small muscles. Gross motor activities such as running, dancing, and riding a tricycle are better than activities that require fine motor skills, such as systematic writing. However, if a child is able and willing, learning to form letters is fine, especially in short, fifteen- to twenty-minute blocks.
- They may be simultaneously mature in one area and immature in others. Development is uneven during this time. One child may be coordinated on the monkey bars at age six but not writing well, and another child the same age may be writing well but not coordinated on the monkey bars. Although there are wide ranges of physical, intellectual, and emotional development at this age, we can relax—things eventually even out!

All of this explains so much about the ways of children in the early years, and it also sheds light on why children this age tend to struggle in a classroom setting. It's difficult for a one-size-fits-all approach to effectively meet the needs of children at different stages of development. A standard curriculum approach has limited flexibility to accommodate the ebb and flow of learning. Some kids may or may not yet be ready to learn certain skills at the point the curriculum dictates they learn those skills. The danger is that trying to teach before children are ready can actually impede their learning.

Did you know that when children are ready, they typically need thirty hours or less of reading instruction?[2] Some children need far less than that. The same is true for math. Leigh Eagar, a former junior high and high school math teacher, noted that elementary math can be learned in eight weeks if we only wait until children are ready to learn it. She believes that if we do, then they are able to retain their natural curiosity about math, and we don't waste precious time drilling them on things they are not developmentally ready to learn.[3] That means we don't have to rush. It's safe, and even preferable, to be unhurried and enjoy the learning process with our kids, because when kids are learning in a pressure-free environment (which parents can easily provide) their learning flourishes.

Another important part of these early years that is foundational to higher learning is allowing generous amounts of playtime. While age-appropriate responsibilities encourage independence and increase confidence, playtime nurtures healthy brain development.[4] Kids are made to move. Again, if we force them to do what is contrary to their individual developmental stage, we not only do them a great disservice, we can actually do damage.

An Abundant Harvest

One of the reasons I wrote *The Unhurried Homeschooler* was because I saw so many parents who once had a relaxed, enjoyable time with their little ones lose it when their kids reached school age. Suddenly, it seemed like a starter pistol had gone off, and they became obsessed with education. But what these parents failed to realize was that their child was already learning a great deal! Because their child's learning was natural and didn't involve a curriculum, they had a hard time seeing it as "real" learning, but nothing could be further from the truth!

What truly broke my heart was the hijacking of the parents' precious time with their kids. Every parent wants to do the right thing, and our culture tells us that early education is the right thing. I couldn't agree more, but I don't think early education has to happen in a classroom setting.

What you are already doing with your child—reading aloud; giving them care, comfort, relief, correction, and guidance through a simple daily routine; and inviting them to engage life with you—*is* educational. You are shaping your child's habits, view of the world, and understanding of right and wrong. You are teaching respect and empathy, building his or her confidence, laying a foundation for higher learning, and countless other essentials.

There is a reason these years are called "the formative years." I love the analogy of starting seeds in a greenhouse, which provides a beautiful parallel to raising kids. The benefit of growing plants from seeds in a greenhouse is that they begin in ideal conditions, which gives them a strong and healthy start. The greenhouse gardener begins with the end—an abundant harvest—in mind.

The gardener first fills small containers with rich soil. Then he carefully plants the seeds, making sure they have just the right amount of water, sunlight, and nutrients. He checks on them frequently. After a while, the soil parts, and tiny seedlings emerge. In the greenhouse, the gardener can protect the fragile plants from harsh weather and any other adverse conditions. This gives seedlings the time they need to grow a healthy root system through which they will draw all their nutrients. Slowly, the seedlings begin to grow into sturdy plants with stalks and foliage, but they're still not quite ready to be moved out of the greenhouse.

Before relocating the plants outdoors, the gardener must acclimate them by putting them outside for short periods of time. This process is called "hardening." The plants will be set outside during the day and brought in at night, or not put out at all if the weather is too harsh. Slowly, under the right amount of weather adversity (not too much), the plants continue to grow and become stronger. The gardener continues to expose them to the elements for longer and longer periods of time until, eventually, the plants are ready to be permanently placed in the outdoor garden.

You can probably already see how the greenhouse analogy parallels raising children. Our children come to us fragile and dependent, and it's our job to nurture their little minds, bodies, and spirits. We protect them from things that might harm them at a tender age. We give them the care they need to grow a strong root system and healthy stalk. And we choose to expose them to the elements when *we* believe they are ready.

Parents, you can decide these things for your children. You can decide how you want to raise and educate them. You are free to make or find the kind of educational experience you want for them.

At the end of your parenting journey, I believe you'll want to look back and have no regrets about the life you chose to live with your kids, for the memories made and the heartstrings tied. It is time well spent.

1. How does providing a simple, consistent routine help our young children?

2. Are there adjustments you could make to your daily life that would create more consistency?

3. What are some daily activities you could invite your child to do with you?

4. Are there daily activities you could encourage your child to do on their own?

5. What new skills might your child be ready for?

6. What skills have they tried but clearly aren't ready for yet?

7. List a few things you know your child has learned without "formal" education (include developmental milestones and responsibilities).

8. What kind of life do you want to have with your kids?

CHAPTER 11

Growing Confidence

The Middle Years

If there is such a thing as a "smooth" season in the home-school years, it often happens during what I call the "middle years," which span the ages of eight to eleven. There is also an important shift that happens during this middle season, one that transitions your child from the early years to being ready for junior high.

The ebb and flow of learning that happens in the early years continues into the middle years. Because different children of the same age will naturally be at different levels of learning, one of the most important ways you can use your parental discernment in this season is to avoid making comparisons. Remember, kids can seem behind but catch up quickly if we simply wait until they are *ready* to learn. If we give in to comparisons, our kids will pick up on our disappointment, which will only create anxiety in them. Kids who are stressed or anxious don't learn well. Wherever they are in their learning, we want our kids to know that we are 100 percent in their corner, that we are a team.

Our children are not our projects. They are unique persons with their own internal clocks that set the pace for their learning and their own thoughts and ideas. If our kids feel like they are our projects, it undermines the confidence we want them to have—the confidence that they *can* learn. In fact, one of the greatest gifts we can give our kids, especially when they're struggling, is a growth mindset.

A Growth Mindset

According to cognitive psychologist Dr. Carol Dweck, people who have a growth mindset "believe that their most basic abilities can be developed through dedication and hard work—brains and talent are just the starting point. This view creates a love of learning and a resilience that is essential for great accomplishment."[1] A growth mindset makes a big difference in how kids interpret and respond to challenges, obstacles, effort, criticism, and the success or failure of others. We can help our kids develop this mindset in any number of ways—through chores, friendships, projects, sports, schoolwork. It's basically a willingness to face obstacles and to not be afraid to fail. Fear of failure can stunt or derail growth, but having a growth mindset opens up endless possibilities!

In order to encourage a love of learning, I first helped my kids develop a growth mindset in areas other than schoolwork, especially early on. If my third grader was struggling in schoolwork, I focused more on growing his perseverance through chores or sports or special projects rather than schoolwork. However, if my sixth grader was struggling, I leaned more heavily toward encouraging perseverance in schoolwork. Here's why. Developmentally, a sixth grader is likely to be more ready for that challenge than a third grader. If my struggling child is overcoming challenges in areas other than schoolwork, resilience and confidence are still developing, and eventually, that child will realize that they can apply that same growth mindset to schoolwork.

The caveat here is that we are talking about *your* child, not mine. Listen to that parental discernment, and do what *you* believe is best for your child. If you make a mistake, there's no shame in changing the game plan. You have that freedom, and your child will respond positively to your willingness to be flexible. In fact, when you admit that something isn't working and find a better way, you are teaching your kids what it looks like to be a lifelong learner, critical thinker, and problem solver.

Discernment in the Middle Years

One discernment challenge for many parents is how to distinguish between a struggle to learn and laziness or resistance. How do we know if we are dealing with a developmental issue or a character issue? When parents ask me about this, I always ask if their child has the same struggle doing their chores or other non-school-related tasks. If so, then I would say it's likely a character issue. However, if the child responds with reluctance only to schoolwork, then it's possible there's an issue with what they are learning or the way they are learning it.

This is a great time to have a conversation about what is and isn't working for your child. For example, sometimes my kids said it was too quiet and they needed music to be able to focus. Other times, they said it was too noisy and they needed quiet. Our boys often needed to be doing something else while they were doing their schoolwork, such as sitting on an exercise ball, reading while hanging upside down from the couch, or taking more breaks for physical activity. We made adjustments, and soon they were back in a good rhythm.

Once again, this is the beauty of home educating—you can take the time to have these conversations. Not only do you learn more about your children, but your children learn more about themselves. This equips them to better understand how they learn, how to recognize when something isn't working, and that there's no need to be afraid of making adjustments when necessary. This, too, is part of having a growth mindset. When we normalize acknowledging struggles and making adjustments, our kids are able to embrace their uniquenesses rather than feel ashamed of them.

None of this would be possible in a classroom setting because of the number of kids, various restrictions, and lack of resources, but *we* can give our kids the freedom to learn in a way that works best for them. When we do, learning is neither stressful nor a drag. It's exciting, fun, and creative. Our kids get to be who God made them to be, and they understand and accept their individuality early on. What a gift!

Watching our kids, having these conversations with them, making adjustments, and working as a team takes time. It's imperative that we continue to keep an unhurried (and thoughtful) heart as we move through these middle years. As opportunities arise, we can slowly encourage more initiative in our kids so that when they reach junior high, they are owning more of their education than ever.

Progress, Not Perfection

By the beginning of these middle years (around age eight), your child is, hopefully, fairly independent in reading, math, and handwriting. They know what they are supposed to do each day, and they move forward without a lot of prodding. Although some may need more support than others, our goal is to continue encouraging independence.

In our family, I was available for questions, but I wanted our kids to know what they needed to do and then do it. Sometimes we used charts to help them stay on track. We also used lots of praise along the way, but not empty praise. We focused on affirming them when they made good decisions, took responsibility and initiative, or owned anything they were doing, whether it was schoolwork or chores.

One thing to keep in mind is that our children aren't going to act or think like adults at this age. We are training them, so we have to continue to hold them accountable. Again, we can apply the principle of, "Don't expect what you aren't willing to inspect." This is why I always inspected chores and schoolwork right after they were finished. I sat down for a few minutes with each child and briefly reviewed their work. Inspection is less about looking for faults and errors and more about looking for things to praise and providing coaching when necessary. You want your child to look forward to inspection, not dread it. This is a time to lean heavy on the side of encouragement for the things they have done well and for progress made. We are shooting for progress, not perfection.

By spending a little time each day, you can keep your finger on the pulse of your child's progress. In addition to preventing any big disasters, daily check-ins help you avoid accumulating piles of paper that take hours to go through at the end of the week. Also, there's nothing worse than going over a week or two of schoolwork only to find out that your child didn't understand a concept at the beginning and that all the work is wrong and has to be redone. It's discouraging for you *and* for your child, which can undermine a healthy mindset toward schoolwork. I can tell you from hindsight that most of what we do to help our kids master the basics at this stage is about plodding along—being consistent in monotonous habits such as checking schoolwork daily.

There were times, especially as the kids reached sixth grade, that they began to push back. Be prepared for that, even from the most compliant child. This can be the beginning of their wanting to cut the apron strings, which is quite natural as they approach junior high. It's healthy as long as it stays within certain boundaries, the main one being that they continue to be respectful to you as their parent, and they understand that most decisions are still yours to make. It's a delicate balance, but honest and respectful conversations can make all the difference.[2]

By the time your kids are in the middle years, there's a good chance you are now more fully aware of both your parenting style and your teaching style. Embrace both by taking them into consideration as you approach your homeschool plan. Your teaching style needs to work for your child, but it also needs to work for you! Sometimes it might feel as though this is counterintuitive, but remember that yours is a God-given role. God can and will help you problem solve and find something that works for you, your child, your family, and your lifestyle.

Writing and the Middle Years

One of the most common learning challenges that arises in the middle years is in regard to writing. I can't tell you how many moms over the years have told me that their child is struggling with writing during this stage. I faced this challenge with some of my kids as well.

First, it's important to know that writing doesn't happen

in a vacuum. The learning environment we create for our kids actually impacts our kids physiologically, which can either enhance or hinder their ability to write. For example, the part of the brain that is associated with speaking and writing is the frontal lobe. This area is also responsible for movement, reasoning, judgment, planning, and problem solving.[3] When a human being is anxious or stressed, the first part of the brain that shuts down is the frontal lobe. This means that if a child is stressed about writing, there will likely be little to no progress. So the key is to keep writing fun and stress-free. Here are five techniques I used to do that with my kids.

Narration

This is a pre-writing exercise during which I read to our kids and then they told me in their own words what they heard, as in, "This happened, then this, then this." This exercise can be used starting at a very young age, and it helps kids develop several skills: comprehension (remembering what they read and the order of events), finding the appropriate words (word retrieval), communication, sentence structure, and so on. The kids also enjoyed having my attention and enthusiasm as I listened and asked questions.

Copywork

The idea here is to familiarize children with good writing—composition, spelling, and punctuation—by having them copy it down. It can be anything from poetry or Bible verses to great literature. The sky is the limit! As our kids do this, they practice handwriting and also learn spelling, punctuation, sentence structure, vocabulary, and grammar. It's also a simple way to expose them to lots of different literature, which is always a great thing!

Dictation

Once the kids had been doing copywork for a while, we moved on to dictation. Instead of copying the writing from the text, I read the text to them, and they wrote it down. This required them to listen, translate words onto paper, spell properly, and use proper punctuation.

By the time they had worked through narration, copywork, and dictation, the kids were ready to write on their own. I'm not saying they didn't do any writing on their own before this, but these exercises often helped their writing tremendously.

Freewriting

I used freewriting to encourage the kids to begin writing their own thoughts. I set a timer for 5–15 minutes and told them to write anything that came to mind. It didn't have to all tie together, and it wasn't corrected for spelling or grammar. It was simply an exercise in getting their thoughts down on paper, because that is a skill in and of itself.

Reading Summaries

Once they were able, I had our kids write a brief summary, or written narration, of what they read each day. This built on the verbal narration exercises described above. Whenever they seemed ready, I had them begin writing one sentence summarizing their reading, then two, and so on. Eventually, they wrote one to two paragraphs a day. They continued to do that throughout most of their school years.

These are just a handful of simple things we did that helped build a foundation for writing. What really accelerated our kids' writing was when they were naturally interested in something, whether that was documenting the life of the animals we owned, writing fictional stories about times in history that they found interesting, or even the "dictionary letters" Jenna wrote to her siblings.

Reading and the Middle Years

Reading can look very different for each child during this season. Some children are reading very well by now and seem to enjoy it, but many may still be struggling, and that's OK. The important thing is not to turn it into a power struggle. The truth is, while we long for our children to love reading because we know it is a valuable tool for ongoing learning, there are some kids who will simply never love it. Some won't love it while growing up, but as adults they find it is a necessary tool to help them accomplish their goals, and then love, or at least appreciation for its benefits, grows.

In the meantime, our job is to continue to gently encourage our kids to read. We can do this in a variety of ways that avoid the power struggle and encourage a positive attitude toward reading. I required our kids to read every day, but if reading was not something they loved, I kept the required reading time to a minimum. Sometimes I allowed reading they did for another subject to count toward required reading time, especially if there was a fair amount of reading in that particular curriculum. Typically, for third through sixth grade, I considered 20–30 minutes of reading a day adequate. Of course, the kids who liked reading naturally read for their own enjoyment in addition to that. Even the child who is reading recipes or instructions for building LEGOs or other projects is reading in addition to the daily requirements.

Audiobooks can be a great tool if you have a struggling reader. Often, our boys needed to move or do something with their hands in order to focus. Some children even find it enjoyable to listen and follow along in their own book.

Another way I encouraged reading was to always have good books lying around, sometimes very strategically. If our kids had mentioned an area of learning that sounded interesting to them or I saw they were intrigued by a specific topic, I picked up books on those topics at the library and made sure they noticed them. If I was at a yard sale or thrift store and ran across books I thought might interest one or more of our children, I'd buy them.

I can't emphasize how important it is to choose books well. Books aren't just informational; they have the potential to help shape our kids' thinking and character. Charlotte Mason, an educator and strong advocate for gentle, natural learning, describes these as "living books":

> Living books are usually written by one person who has a passion for the subject and writes in conversational or narrative style. The books pull you into the subject and involve your emotions, so it's easy to remember the events and facts. Living books make the subject "come alive." They can be contrasted to dry writing, like what is found in most encyclopedias or textbooks, which basically lists informational facts in summary form.[4]

A quick browse on the internet provides many book lists that qualify as "living." The story-like content in these books make it easier for children to understand. In addition, living books help our kids master foundational learning skills. Sarah Mackenzie tells us in *The Read-Aloud Family*:

> We need our kids to fall in love with stories before they are even taught their first letters, if possible, because everything else—phonics, comprehension, analysis, even writing—comes so much more easily when a child loves books.[5]

Living books can also help us gently incorporate subjects like history, science, and geography that can otherwise often feel somewhat dry and boring into our days.

You might be under the impression that the third-to-sixth grader has outgrown the read-aloud stage, but nothing could be further from the truth! When we slow down and take time to partake in a story as a family, we create a sense of community and camaraderie. Sharing a book together gives us something to talk about and relate to. Reading together lends itself to a closeness that can be difficult to accomplish any other way.

Sometimes reading aloud can be an exercise in patience if we have several children, especially if we have young children. It helps to have something for little hands to do while we are reading, especially for boys, who tend to be in perpetual motion. Allowing younger kids to be excused after a certain amount of time while you continue reading with older kids can also be helpful. There are many approaches we can take to create a reading ritual for our families. If you're interested in learning more on this subject, I highly recommend *The Read-Aloud Family* by Sarah Mackenzie.

Math

Math is often the bane of our existence as homeschool parents and the subject we most fear teaching. There can be many reasons for math phobia, from our own struggles to bad experiences with poor teachers. I am far from being a math guru, but I did discover two things that made teaching math easier for me. First, there aren't as many new math concepts taught each year as we might think. Most concepts from the previous year are revisited the next year with only a few new concepts introduced. Second, there are many great math programs that make teaching math easier. It's often a matter of finding what works best for your child.

As I mentioned in the previous chapter, Leigh Eagar, a former junior high and high school math teacher, said that when a child is ready to learn, all of elementary math can be taught in eight weeks, so we really *can* relax. If we are not looking for perfection but progress, we can gently keep moving forward without getting stressed out and unintentionally passing on our math fears to our kids.

I always believed my main job was to make sure my kids knew the basics: addition, subtraction, multiplication, division, fractions, decimals, percentages, and measurements. With those concepts firmly in place, they could learn any level of upper-level math they might need for college or a job. Most of my kids didn't need to learn anything beyond the basics, and those who did chose to because they either loved math or were motivated by a goal they were trying to reach, such as a college degree. At that point, they owned the progress they needed to make in order to reach their goals.

Kids in the middle years also learn math concepts simply by engaging in everyday life: using measuring utensils while cooking, using a tape measure for building projects, practicing music, and through countless other hobbies and projects in which they have an interest. Again, if they are motivated to accomplish a goal, they will learn whatever they need to learn in order to reach that goal. They can also learn upper-level math concepts from logic games, puzzles, brain games, and so on. Never underestimate the value of LEGOs! Our boys played LEGOs for countless hours, and it turns out that some pretty impressive math concepts—from basic fractions to square numbers—can be learned through playing with LEGOs.[6]

So take a deep breath and relax. Like every other subject, you don't have to know everything about math in order for your child to be able to grow in their skills. There are plenty of helpful websites out there. With your encouragement and praise, your kids can develop a growth mindset in this subject as well.

Play

Play is still essential during the middle years, although it begins to look less like play and more like time spent on interests and hobbies, especially as our kids near junior high age. They need time each day to pursue the things they are interested in. This time is important in order to reset the brain and pave the way for learning. In order to protect this time, we need to be as efficient as possible with the time we devote to schoolwork.

It is reasonable to expect that schoolwork during the middle years can be accomplished in anywhere from ninety minutes (in the younger middle years) to two-and-a-half or three hours (in the older middle years). Much depends on the child and the approach you decide to take, but in a home environment, the teacher-to-child ratio is better than ideal. Plus, almost all other negative variables that exist in a traditional classroom are eliminated. You are well positioned for success!

Here are some time-savers I've discovered that can help make your kids' learning time even more efficient:

- **Eliminate distractions.** Turn off all cell phones, gadgets, and any other potential interruptions so everyone can focus.
- **Have your children correct their own work.** For example, you might use workbooks that have an answer key.

Of course, you will need to double-check their work, but it will take less time if they review it first. Many times, children learn more from correcting their own work than by having you correct it for them.

- **Combine subjects.** For example, you might combine reading and spelling by choosing spelling and vocabulary words from that day's reading. If you read something on the topic of history or a biography of a historical figure, you have covered history as well as reading.

- **Teach one subject to different ages simultaneously.** Along that same line, if you have children of multiple ages, do as much as you can together. You might combine pre-reading for one child with writing for an older child by having the younger child do narration while the older child takes dictation or writes a summary. You can also purchase unit studies to accomplish teaching across age levels. Gather 'Round Homeschool is one of my favorites resources for this.

- **Use a timer.** This is especially helpful for kids who tend to drag their feet. It's like they need a little bit of pressure to be motivated. I often let them tell me how long they think it might take them to accomplish something to avoid pressuring them with my opinion. It accomplishes two things: they learn more about time management, and they are forced to own more of what they are doing. The only caveat is that sometimes kids are distracted because they need a brain break. You may have to experiment and use your parental discernment, but either way, using a timer will help make their learning time more efficient and eliminate the need to nag them, which pretty much sucks the life out of everyone.

One other thing our family did during the early and middle years that made our school time more efficient was not requiring the *formal* study of history or science. (If you just gasped in horror, hang in there with me while I explain.) I decided to take this approach because when I thought back over my years in school, I remembered little to none of the history or science that was formally taught in kindergarten through sixth grade. I don't think I'm exceptional in that regard. Developmentally, kids aren't typically ready to fully process the many nuances of either of those subjects. However, I do believe there are great benefits to exposing kids to history and science and we can accomplish these subjects through family life naturally, via activities like reading interesting stories about key historical figures, visiting a historical site or museum, cooking, or observing the weather. We always had living books lying around on weather, geology, astronomy, how things work, natural disasters, and historical periods and how people lived, as well as biographies and books of simple science experiments. You get the idea. Often, specific topics would come up in conversation, and if the kids' interest was piqued, we would pull out books on the topic from our home library or the public library. They also watched educational programming such as *The Magic School Bus*, *Wild Kratts*, *Liberty's Kids*, and documentaries.

When our kids were in junior high, we still made history and science optional, but often, those subjects had become particularly interesting to them, and they wanted to pursue a more formal study.

It wasn't until high school that we required the study of history and science. By then, they were more engaged and had the ability to understand scientific concepts and how historical events tied together. Because their brains were more developed, they were able to take in more information and see how it all fit in the bigger picture.

This approach may not be right for everyone, but it worked well for our family. If you find your kids love science or history, and you can teach most of their subjects from that place of interest, you should absolutely do that! Or, if you simply aren't comfortable not doing *something* in those subjects, you can devote time to them a few days a week.

Solidify Your Relationship

What I love most about the middle years is that our kids are now old enough to communicate what is working well for them and what is not. Our conversations can be more in depth as they are able to think through things more logically. We can encourage them to own more and more of their life and education by pointing out cause and effect for their choices.

We are still the parents, and we are responsible for all final decisions, but it's important to build relationships with our children by establishing trust and open, respectful communication. Invite them into problem-solving and healthy discussions about decisions that need to be made. This will communicate a sense of teamwork and prepare us to walk through the teen years with a solid foundation intact.

In any season of parenting or homeschooling, I always caution parents to remain vigilant against filling their calendars with too many activities. The simple, unhurried, and unplanned moments with your kids are where the most important connections happen. These are often the greatest moments of influence. If you are hurried and overly busy, it's much more likely that these opportunities will be less beneficial or overlooked completely. It's essential that you keep your head in the game, staying connected to what is actually working for your family and saying no to what is not.

Home education gives you the freedom to do just that. You are not stuck in a one-size-fits-all format. Your approach can be as creative and unique as your family!

The most important thing is that you enjoy the journey by engaging with your kids and creating an environment that encourages lifelong learning by providing a warm, loving, safe, secure family life.

1. In what ways can you encourage a growth mindset in your child? How about in yourself?

2. Can you see areas in which your child needs to grow or take more initiative? Through what parts of daily life could you encourage that growth?

3. Have you had a conversation lately with your child, asking them about what is going well and what seems to be a struggle for them? If not, consider doing so.

4. Are you keeping a good pulse on where your child is physically, mentally, emotionally, and spiritually? If not, how can you do this regularly?

5. If you are experiencing pushback from your child, what kinds of questions could you ask in a relaxed setting that would help them problem solve? (Hint: Ask, then listen to understand. Don't just reply. You want your child to experience and own the process.)

6. Is your child comfortable writing out their thoughts and feelings? If so, consider encouraging them to do this.

CHAPTER 12

The Sky's the Limit

The Final School Years

We referred to them as the "just-you-waits." These were the things people said when they saw my husband and me with our small children and felt the need to warn us: "Just you wait until they are teenagers." It was as if our cute, respectful, well-behaved children would turn thirteen and suddenly become teen demons.

Now that we're on the other side of raising seven of our eight kids, I can tell you the teen years have been by far some of the *best* years with our kids. However, these years were also full of many transitions that were both exciting and frightening, for us as well as our kids, and it was not always smooth sailing. In fact, there were times I thought I might lose my sanity—not because our kids were a big problem, but because walking alongside them during this season required *me* to stretch and grow. Was it worth it? Absolutely! But in order to successfully navigate these uncharted waters, we had to make relationships with our teens a priority.

Transitioning Your Approach to Parenting

Do you remember what it was like to be a teenager? Do you remember how quickly your body was changing and how hard it was to keep up, or how unsure you were of yourself? Do you remember the overwhelming pressures you felt then that now seem so unimportant?

Our kids are walking through all of that, along with their own unique struggles, and what they need most is for us to strive consistently for a good relationship with them. This doesn't mean we stop being parents. It just means we transition into more of a coaching and consulting role.

Unfortunately, many parents do the opposite. They may have parented loosely when their kids were young, and then switch gears and suddenly try to rein in their kids during the teen years. This is often a knee-jerk response to preconceived notions that teens are inevitably lazy, disrespectful, and irresponsible. It can be a particular challenge for parents who had a tumultuous time as teens themselves, and they react from a place of fear that their teens will make the same mistakes they did.

I can tell you from experience that it doesn't have to be this way. God has a much better plan. In his book, *Age of Opportunity: A Biblical Guide to Parenting Teens,* Paul Tripp writes, "You are called to be an instrument of wisdom in your teenager's life. To do so, you must be gentle, humble, patient and persevering."[1] A certain amount of self-sacrifice is unavoidable if we want to invest well in this final season of our children being home and finish well.

These years are the culmination of all the work we've done to reverse engineering our kids' education. As our kids move toward graduation and adulthood, we want them to take full ownership of their lives, including their education.

One of the ways Darryl and I did this was to explain to the kids, when they were still in junior high, that once they got into high school, they would be responsible to meet the graduation requirements we had agreed upon. We encouraged them to mentally prepare themselves for that. We assured them that we would be available to discuss options, provide resources, and give counsel if needed, but ultimately, they were responsible. We wanted them to know that when they walked across the stage to receive their high school diploma, they would have the confidence of knowing it was *their* accomplishment. We encouraged them to shore up any study habits they might need to help them be prepared, and to put more effort into any subjects in which they wanted to become more confident. In this conversation, we also asked questions such as these, which were helpful when we were ready to plan for high school:

What do you feel really good at?
In what areas would you like to improve?
Are there any subjects you'd like to learn more about?
Do you feel like you are ready for high school? Why or why not?
How can we help you meet your goals?
How can we best support and love you right now?

It's amazing what you can learn by asking a few questions!

Think of junior high as a transitional time between elementary school and high school, but bear in mind that sometimes, that transition continues into the first or even second year of high school. Don't panic. Be patient, be encouraging, and consistently pray for God to be working in the heart of your child, helping them grow at just the right pace and bringing the right experiences into their lives in his timing.

I always say that God is never in a hurry, but he's also never late.

It's possible that some of the skills you hoped your child would learn before they graduated won't actually be learned until adulthood, and that's OK. The right motivation at the right time does wonders. Your job is to love them consistently through it all. Sometimes that means challenging them, while other times it means helping them adjust their course, encouraging them, or simply praying hard for them.

Before our kids were in high school, when people found out that we homeschooled, I can't tell you how many of them said, "You aren't going to keep homeschooling through high school, are you?" What they didn't realize was that by saying this, they were actually cementing my determination to do just that.

I had no intention of investing years of our lives in encouraging a love of learning in our kids, as well as nurturing a growing sense of self and a strong bond with family, only to toss them into a system which, I believed, would most likely undermine that investment. I'm not saying that's the best decision for every family, but I knew in my gut it was the best for mine.

There are many ways to navigate the high school journey, and I hope that by now you feel free to keep the options open for your kids for as long as possible. I realize that this is almost the opposite of what many of us experienced in a traditional school setting, but we have to ask ourselves why we would want to limit the definition of educational success to just one path. Each child is uniquely gifted. Their gifts deserve to be recognized and acknowledged as valuable. There are so many different ways to succeed!

Encouraging Ownership in High School

For many years, we were involved in a homeschool program that allowed us to educate our kids at home using the methods we believed were best and gave them the opportunity to attend extracurricular classes at a local school. When our kids were in high school, they also had the opportunity to earn an official high school diploma from our local school district. To do so, we were required to turn in brief monthly progress reports and to meet with a consultant once a month.

One of the ways we encouraged ownership in our high schoolers was to have them write their own monthly progress reports and meet with the consultant one-on-one. By this time, I had a solid relationship with the consultant. She knew our family, and we shared the same perspective on education, so I knew I could trust her to meet with our kids one-on-one. She approved all of the progress reports and entered the kids' grades into the district's record system at the end of each semester.

We used the district's course credit requirements as our goal, but we met them in ways that worked best for each of our kids. Our kids were also required to do some testing in order to earn their diplomas. I'm not a fan of testing, especially in the early years, but high school kids are usually developmentally ready for challenges such as learning how to do well on a standardized test. It's also easier for them to understand that a test is not a defining measure of intelligence, whereas younger children aren't always developmentally capable of processing test results without their confidence being undermined.

We found it helpful to have our high schoolers accountable to someone other than us for parts of their education. This happened when they attended classes in person or online, and it created a healthy kind of pressure that moved them toward ownership of what they were learning.

Five of our kids earned their diplomas through this partnership with the local school district, but then we moved across the country, and everything changed. The only option for extracurricular classes in our new home was to take them at the local high school, which neither of our teens wanted to do.

Instead, they decided to get jobs and work part-time while finishing high school. This was something they initiated, and it turned out to have multiple benefits. Not only did they start to "adult" early on, they learned new skills that could be translated into high school credits. We were still accomplishing the goal of having them be accountable to someone else; it just happened in a work setting rather than a classroom setting.

To start, I found a blank transcript online and printed out two copies of it. I then took my two teens out for coffee and had them transfer the credits they had earned up to that point from their former homeschool program onto these new, blank transcripts. I didn't do it for them. I gave them a little guidance when needed, and when they were finished, we had a relaxed conversation about what they needed to accomplish to earn their diplomas. I asked many of the questions listed above, and by the time we were finished, they knew where they were headed and how they planned to get there. Completing their transcripts was an opportunity to encourage ownership, and I took full advantage of it.

Keeping the End in Mind

Even as our kids become high schoolers, we have to continue to keep the end in mind, keeping open as many options as possible. One of the ways we do this is by translating our kids' interests into credits. To give you an idea of what that might look like, here are some examples.

Turning Interests into Credits

Brittney, our oldest, loved animals. Over the years, she owned an entire menagerie that included sheep, goats, horses, ponies, chickens, a milking cow, dogs, and cats. She educated herself on the anatomy and habits of each animal as well as how to care for it. She kept detailed records on each animal, often making daily entries. She read countless books on a variety of topics concerning animals. As part of her high school transcript, we counted these experiences toward animal science, reading, and several electives.

Brittney also loved learning about the personality traits of people (such as Hippocrates' four temperaments: choleric, sanguine, melancholic, and phlegmatic), as well as learning about love languages and giftings. Depending on the resources she utilized, she could earn credits toward personal development,[2] which fell under physical education and health discipline in most schools. She could also have taken credits for an introduction to psychology class, which would likely have been a social sciences elective credit.

When one of our sons worked part-time at Chick-fil-A—a company known for its courteous, well-trained employees—I knew he was learning a myriad of skills on the job. I had him describe in detail what he did at work so we could translate that effectively into credits. Some of the credits he earned were food service preparation and regulation, customer and employee relations, business principles, and interpersonal communication.

During that same time, he also spent weekends lending a helping hand to a friend who was building a house. Since he was developing skills there as well, we listed those under "student achievement and skills." This was simply an extra category added to his transcript, as he didn't spend enough hours doing this to warrant a full or half credit.

The point is, everything counts! Whatever interests your kids have, or whatever life skills they want or need to learn, they can earn credits in those areas. This is a key factor that makes home educating so efficient and effective!

Another benefit is that credits for certain subjects can be combined. For instance, when one of our son's course load felt like it was becoming too heavy, I combined writing and history by having him read the history text and write a summary of what he had read that day. This is especially helpful if a young person has other interests they are passionate about. We can encourage them to pursue their interests and insert core subjects (reading, writing, and math) along the way.

Core Curriculum

Each state has different rules and regulations for home education, so it's important to pay attention to those and honor them. Just remember that you can often use a more innovative approach than you might realize. Be creative, and think outside the box.

You may wonder what constitutes a credit. I wondered the same thing.

In the state we lived in previously, one credit was approximately 170 hours, which essentially equaled one of the following:

- Completing a textbook
- Completing a course (online or DVD)
- Attending/completing a class in person

I typically had several resources already picked out for my kids to choose from. There were one or two approaches I was fairly insistent on, because I was keeping the big picture in mind. History was one of those.

As I mentioned previously, until high school, I allowed our kids to engage in interest-led learning when it came to history. What worked best for us was utilizing opportunities and/or books that interested the kids along with many random conversations as various topics in history naturally came up. Simple exposure along the way seemed to be enough. When our kids entered high school, though, I knew their minds were ready to take in more and make lasting connections. I wanted them to have a bird's-eye view of how world history and biblical history were intertwined. I wanted them to see God's hand weaving together the intricate details and to learn the life lessons and wisdom that studying history can provide. I highly recommended a program called The Mystery of History, which is a Christian world history curriculum. I didn't force it on my kids, and not every one of them chose to use it, but most of them did. I think it helped when I explained both my passion for it and the reasons I wanted them to use it. Ultimately, however, I left it up to them.

We approached science the same way. There were plenty of "experiments" that happened at our house, and a variety of natural conversations that were science-related, but unless they showed a particular interest in that subject, we saved the programs and full curriculum for the upper grades.

Keeping Options Open

As a high schooler, Luke was interested in becoming a physical therapist. He chose to use a textbook on anatomy to meet one of his science requirements, but before he invested more time and energy into pursuing this career, we thought it might be a good idea for him to job shadow. We contacted a local physical therapy office and explained what we were looking for. They were happy to oblige. We have found that nearly 100 percent of the time, people are happy to share their professions with an interested young person, especially young people who are attentive, helpful, and respectful.

It only took one day for Luke to realize that the job of a physical therapist was not what he wanted to do. He wanted to spend most of his time working directly with patients, but he discovered a lot of time was spent doing paperwork. At that point, it was still easy to redirect his career path, but what if he had wasted several years, as well as money and effort, pursuing something that ultimately wasn't what he wanted to be doing? He would have felt stuck in a career he didn't enjoy and most likely burdened with college debt that would take him years to pay off.

There is so much pressure for kids to decide their career path in high school. Most of the time, that just isn't realistic. If kids have been allowed to pursue their interests throughout elementary and high school, there is a good chance they will at least narrow down their interests. Sometimes they simply need more time, and that is OK. This makes sense given the fact that their brains aren't fully developed. According to neuroscientist Sandra Aamodt, this doesn't happen until age twenty-five. "The changes that happen between eighteen and twenty-five are a continuation of the process that starts around puberty," she writes, "and eighteen-year-olds are about halfway through that process. Their prefrontal cortex is not yet fully developed. That's the part of the brain that helps you to inhibit impulses and to plan and organize your behavior to reach a goal."[3] This doesn't mean young adults can't make life decisions before age twenty-five; it just means they may need more time and encouragement from us in order to choose well.

After our kids graduated from high school, we encouraged them to continue exploring their interests while also being gainfully employed. They could live fairly cheaply at home if they wanted to, but if they weren't in school full-time, they had to pay something toward rent and food. They would also have a few responsibilities around the house simply because that's real life: we pay bills, and we have responsibilities at home.

It has always surprised me that schools don't require "real-life" subjects, such as decision-making, time management, or consumer math, in order to graduate from high school. For most young people, those topics would be a far wiser investment than algebra or calculus. Since we are raising our kids to be adults, it only makes sense that they should learn to make decisions and manage their time and money well. This is yet another example of educating our kids with the end in mind.

We never had problems related to our kids not adulting well. They wanted to be as independent as possible as soon as possible, not because they didn't love us or want to be around us, but because they had a natural drive, determination, and a desire to move forward with their lives. We raised them to own their lives, and that's exactly what they have done.

There are so many advantages to approaching the high

school years with an open heart and open hands. When we remember that there are countless roads to success, and we consistently help our kids keep open as many options as possible until their desired direction becomes clear, they have the best chance to reach their greatest potential. They can walk through these years with excitement, passion, and a strong sense that the sky's the limit! As parents, it's a privilege to walk alongside our kids as they transition into adulthood, spread their wings, and take flight.

REAL-LIFE APPLICATION

1. What are a few things that frighten you about raising teens?

2. In what areas are you still parenting where you should be coaching? How can you begin to transition to more consultation and fewer directives?

3. What are some ways you could encourage your teen to own more of their life?

4. What interests does your teen have that could be translated into credits?

5. If your teen has an interest they may want to pursue as a possible career, what are some potential opportunities you could seek out (such as job shadowing)?

6. Are you and your teen purposing to keep open hands and an open heart toward future possibilities? If not, how can you do a better job of this?

CHAPTER 13

The Nature of Things

Over the last thirty years of parenting and twenty-five years of homeschooling, I've watched in wonder the differences between how our five boys took in and processed information versus how our three girls did so. As time passed, I grew even more amazed at how our Creator made each gender with certain tendencies that are beautiful in their own ways.

"Equal but different" has always been my mantra when it comes to recognizing the differences between boys and girls. I realize that these differences really can have a broad range and they aren't cut in stone. However, knowing that boys and girls have certain tendencies helps tremendously when home educating our kids. Remember, we are educating the *whole* child, so respecting how they are hardwired by their Creator is an integral part of that.

Considering the Nature of Boys

I'm going to spend a disproportionate amount of time on boys in this chapter, because I think boys have gotten a bad rap. From the time they are very young, they seem to have boundless energy. They also seem to be hell-bent on killing themselves. As a mother of boys, some days I felt like my biggest parenting and homeschooling accomplishment was that they were all still alive by the end of it!

I once had a conversation with a young mom who complained that her kindergarten son couldn't keep still in class. As though I had a very important secret to tell, I leaned in closely and whispered, "I can tell you exactly why." She looked surprised, but not more surprised than when I said, "It's because he *knows* he is supposed to be chasing frogs and digging in the dirt."

The traditional classroom setting leans heavily in favor of how girls tend to be wired. Because of this, I firmly believe a classroom setting is one of the worst places we can send our sons, especially in the early years. This isn't because teachers are not wonderful, but because little, if anything, in a classroom setting is conducive to the energy and curiosity of little boys. I am not saying that boys should never be required to sit in one place or be quiet, but this is something that's usually learned best in short increments, especially at first.

I'm also not saying that little boys aren't smart enough to do well in school at that age. What I *am* saying is that the traditional classroom is rarely a setting in which young boys thrive. Boys have a fierce need to expend energy. When they have the opportunity to do so, it resets their brains, and they tend to be more cooperative—and much more ready to learn. It's like priming the pump.

Throughout the early years, our boys often did bookwork in shorter increments, depending on their age and stage of development, with breaks between those increments that helped awaken their ability to learn. Physical activities like jumping on a trampoline and running around the outside of the house gave their bodies and brains a boost of oxygen and activated their vestibular (balance) system, which is part of the sensory system. With this in mind, I made taking breaks between subjects or tasks a part of their routine. Knowing they would get a break also motivated them to complete the work at hand. Sometimes they were ready for a break earlier or later than planned, so I had to be tuned in to when they were doing well and could keep moving forward, or when the proverbial lights were on, but no one was home, and it was time for a break. The break might be 3–5 minutes or as long as 10–15 minutes, depending on what they needed at the time.

I confess, I sometimes forgot about them during a break because I was busy with household chores or helping the other kids with their schoolwork. That's when I decided using a timer would be a good idea.

You may wonder how I knew that taking breaks would be beneficial in educating boys. To start with, I grew up during a time when the culture wasn't questioning the fact that boys were boys and girls were girls. Whether someone believed in a Creator or not, gender was almost universally accepted, so I watched my parents and teachers and learned some things along the way.

More than a Teacher

I attended a small country school for many of my elementary years. There were less than 100 kids in kindergarten through eighth grade, so our junior high class of about fifteen students consisted of both seventh and eighth graders.

My teacher, Mr. Clancy, had served in the Navy and was also a dad. I learned a lot from how he handled the classroom, especially the boys. Mr. Clancy had a knack for knowing when the boys were getting restless or stirring up trouble. He sometimes called a few of them to walk outside with him. They'd head across the playground to the back of the school property, which was still within eyeshot of the classroom. He'd hand them shovels and a measuring tape and tell them to dig a four-foot square and four-foot deep hole. The boys would enthusiastically start digging, because anything was better than being stuck in the classroom.

Awhile later, they'd show up sweaty but satisfied that they had conquered their task. Mr. Clancy would walk back out to inspect the project, using the measuring tape to make sure the hole was exactly four feet square and four feet deep. Then he'd tell them it looked great and to fill it back up.

You're probably gasping right now. Fortunately, the statute of limitations has passed, and no one can arrest Mr. Clancy for misconduct. However, the truth is that we could use more of this kind of thinking when it comes to growing kids who have grit.

I can assure you that those kids were not damaged in any way by this. We all knew Mr. Clancy loved his students, had their best interests in mind, and would never do anything to hurt them. He had a good relationship with each and every one. I can't tell you how many letters he has received over the years from grateful students who benefitted from his leadership. There were countless kids who came from very rough homes but became productive, successful adults because Mr. Clancy understood what they needed. For some, he was the first person in their lives who believed in them and helped them realize their worth. He did this not by being proficient at teaching (although he was a good teacher), but by providing a stable and secure learning environment with clear boundaries and expectations. He also understood what kids that age actually need, particularly boys.

In addition to watching Mr. Clancy, I learned about productive ways to engage boys by watching my mom handle my brother's energy with respect for his boyness. Like many boys, when my brother had pent-up energy, he teased and provoked my mom or me. Instead of making him sit in a corner or lecturing him, my mom sent him out to play or made him run around the outside of the house. Of course, he had to ring both the front and back doorbells as he made the ten rounds she required, which allowed him to continue his torture as we listened to the doorbell ring twenty times. But my mom didn't get mad. She thought it was hilarious and still talks about it. In her mind, my brother's boyish ways were a good thing. She took delight in them, which, in turn, made my brother comfortable with being who God made him to be.

God Called It "Good"

Culture bears down hard on men, and it starts when they are very young. Instead of embracing who God created them to be and seeing the incredible potential that their energetic and conquering natures possess, they are continually told in no uncertain terms that what comes naturally for them is bad, and they should essentially be more like girls. By the time these boys reach middle school and high school, all that's left are unmotivated, confused, insecure, and often hopeless young men.

Jordan Peterson, a clinical psychologist and author of several books, including *Twelve Rules for Life*, put it succinctly when he argued that there is a "crisis of masculinity" in which the "masculine spirit is under assault."[1]

As Christian parents, it's crucial we remember that in order for our kids to become all that God has called them to be, we must raise them with a biblical mindset. This means we should always bear in mind that they have a Creator who formed them with certain tendencies that are meant to be a blessing to the people in their lives and to society.

The Bible says God made human beings male and female and called them "good." Men and women were made to complement one another. Their roles are equal but different by intention. It was God's good plan to create men and women to work together in a mutually beneficial relationship that would bring glory and honor to him and be a blessing to each generation.

God's plan was and still is *good*. Unfortunately, our culture is becoming increasingly hostile toward God and his ways. As believers, our decision to follow his ways over the ways of the world requires more and more determination, but I can tell you it's worth it. After all, who really knows best? Wouldn't the designer and creator of something know what is best for what he created? Parents, we can trust in God's good design for our boys and our girls. And sometimes that requires making changes in ourselves.

When we had four teen boys in the house, there was a point at which I had grown increasingly frustrated. It seemed as though our boys heard little or nothing when I spoke. I even questioned whether or not words were actually making it out of my mouth because they were clearly *not* being heard.

Darryl and I went out for dinner one night during this time, and I unloaded my frustrations while he patiently listened. We paid for our meal, and as we were driving out of the parking lot, Darryl said he needed to tell me something, but he didn't want to hurt my feelings. I'd experienced so much relief in being able to voice my frustrations over dinner, though, that I was ready to hear whatever he had to say. In fact, I was all ears.

"You need to use fewer words," he said, tenderly but matter-of-factly. "The more words you use, the less the boys respect you."

Suddenly, the light turned on. It was exactly what I needed to hear, and it resonated with my heart.

I went home and talked to the boys about it. I told them what their dad had said, and they told me they would rather deal with physical consequences such as extra chores or push-ups than to have to listen to more words.

It wasn't easy, but I worked hard to reduce the number of words I used, and the results were astounding. The fact that I had to pause in order to do this well also helped me problem solve a little better. It's amazing how even a slight delay before responding and a reduction in the number of words I spoke helped me be more intentional in my directives.

The same seemed to hold true for schoolwork. The boys preferred that I let them know up front what was expected of them each day and let them follow through independently. Often, they didn't even ask questions when they ran into issues. When I saw them struggling and offered help, they seemed irritated and told me they wanted to figure it out on their own. Sometimes they let me make suggestions, but most of the time, they preferred I didn't. I was never 100 percent sure whether or not this was a good thing, but I decided to respect it. I can now say that our boys became problem solvers and critical thinkers, and I'm pretty convinced that their determination to do things themselves is what most contributed to that.

Equal but Different

Darryl calls me the master of asking questions. I learned early on that when I asked more questions, our kids engaged more, which encouraged ownership. The more they had to answer questions, the more invested they became in the conversation and the topic.

I did this with our boys, but conversations tended to last longer with the girls. Our girls tended to like a curriculum that was wordier; the boys, not so much. There are always exceptions, but this was the overall norm for our kids.

I realize that every child is different and, as I said before, there is a wide range when it comes to the tendencies of girls and boys. Our oldest daughter would probably have been considered a tomboy. She liked being outside with her animals and couldn't have cared less about hair or makeup until much later in her teen years. I think she wore a ponytail until she was fourteen or fifteen. She is now thirty, has been married for eight years, has four kids, and loves being a mom. She has embraced her womanhood but is also very comfortable with who she is because she was allowed to be just that—*who God created her to be.*

As a family, we respected God's design by accepting that boys and girls are different but equal and that this is a beautiful thing. We didn't tell our girls they could do anything a boy could do or vice versa. We simply set them free to be who God designed them to be because that design is beautiful. It's beautiful because God is *good* and has *good* in mind for his people. The popular notion that we have to try to be something we were never created to be and tell our kids to do the same is ludicrous.

While encouraging both the masculine and feminine tendencies of our kids, it's imperative that we don't use masculinity or femininity as excuses for foolishness. The old adage, "Boys will be boys" has been overused to justify negative character issues that must be addressed rather than tolerated.

There is a difference between childishness and foolishness. For example, if our son accidentally spills a glass of milk at the dinner table but was not doing anything disobedient, that would be childishness. However, if he spills a glass of milk while being rowdy, and we have warned him (either in the moment or repeatedly in the past), that is foolishness. He did not heed our warning, and he should experience an appropriate correction (even though boys naturally tend to be rowdier).

The same is true for girls. Sometimes we hear or use excuses such as, "She is just sensitive," when the reality is that the entire household is constantly on edge because no one knows when they might set off an emotional upheaval.

Boundaries are important for both boys and girls. The psalmist wrote:

> LORD, you alone are my portion and my cup;
>   you make my lot secure.
> The boundary lines have fallen for me in pleasant
>   places;
>   surely I have a delightful inheritance. (Psalm
>   16:5–6 NIV)

God puts boundaries around us for *our good*. The same is true when parents set boundaries. So while we respect the differences between boys and girls and allow grace at times for those differences, we do not allow the natural tendencies of boys and girls to stand as excuses for poor character or behavior. In fact, being aware of the differences between boys and girls allows us to exercise grace *while* correcting our kids.

For example, suppose my six-year-old boy tackles his four-year-old sister, and she falls down and starts to cry. I can comfort the four-year-old while calmly asking the six-year-old what he was trying to do. As I ask questions, it will become clear whether or not his motive was to hurt her. My experience is that more often than not, it was impulsivity that drove the boy. He may have been playing with a friend on another occasion (likely another boy) and discovered the art of tackling. It was so much fun for him and his friend, he thought his sister might enjoy the game as well. Unfortunately, he was mistaken, and hopefully there is some remorse for accidentally hurting his sister. All of this can be discovered and handled appropriately in the moment without breaking the boy's spirit or demeaning what comes naturally for him, which in this case is physical play.

Likewise, I can explain to the shell-shocked four-year-old that her brother loves her and thought she might like playing a game he played with his friend, and he didn't mean to hurt her. He can apologize and give her a hug. She can say she forgives him, and before you know it, everyone is as good as new.

The point is, in every conflict we face that involves our children, it is wise to bear in mind that parts or most of a conflict can be attributed to the sometimes vast differences between boys and girls.

Free to Be

In his book *The Minds of Boys*, Michael Gurian shows brain scans of a boy and a girl, both of whom were the same age and both of whom were at rest. The differences between them are remarkable—there was significantly more activity in the female brain.[2] It's a powerful visual of how differently boys and girls respond to the same experience. It also helps explain why it is typical for a young boy to be six to twelve months behind in development compared to girls his own age. They all catch up eventually, but in their own way and according to their own internal clock.

Unfortunately, when their boys struggle in school, too many parents feel as though there is something terribly wrong when the reality is that our educational system has set up boys for failure. Boys are brilliant, funny, creative, determined, and full of life. These characteristics may be revealed in ways we never expected, but mark my words, if you begin to look for it, you *will* see it. When you do, you'll find the keys to unlocking an educational experience that will far surpass anything you could have ever imagined.

Awhile back, I was speaking to a large group of moms. My topic was not boys, but for some reason, I felt compelled to comment on the wonder of boys. I reminded the moms that their boys were created for great things, that their nature was meant to be a blessing, and that God had extraordinary plans for them. I encouraged them to defend their boys' right to be a boy and to allow them to learn and grow in ways that work best for them. I encouraged them to trust that their sons' education could and should be forged in and through their boyness. I assured them that at the end of the journey, not only would their boys be fine, but they would be far better off for it.

When I finished my comments, I saw tears running down the faces of many moms in the room. It was as though someone had set them free to love their boys the way their hearts desperately wanted to but had been prevented from doing because of what they had been told about education and boys.

I want that same freedom for you. God's ways and boundaries were never intended to enslave us, but to set us free. They help us grow strong, healthy families. Healthy family life is a top priority for any Christian family, because everything that flows from the family permanently shapes our children and their character. Home education gives us even more time and opportunities for this. Protecting and defending God's design by being mindful and thankful for the differences between boys and girls, and encouraging our kids to do the same, is one of the most powerful ways we can do this.

REAL-LIFE APPLICATION

For moms of boys:

1. In what ways can you adjust your days to better fit the needs of your son?

2. What would you say are the best qualities about the nature of boys?

3. Are there ways you can better protect your son from the damaging "crisis of masculinity" that is permeating our culture?

4. Do you think it would be helpful if you used fewer words with your son?

5. Can you more easily recognize the difference between foolishness and childishness?

CHAPTER 14

Your Reality

Educating from Where You Live

It was Easter Sunday and we had just eaten a big after-church meal with my in-laws. No sooner were they driving away than we found ourselves in the kitchen, banding our baby goat and giving him a shot of antibiotics.

Darryl looked at me and said, "I can honestly say I never saw this coming, but I wouldn't change a thing!"

We both laughed, because caring for farm animals was not at all how Darryl had been raised. In fact, when I met him, he was a twenty-eight-year-old bachelor who was pretty set in his ways. He grew up in the suburbs with some access to open land at the edge of his neighborhood, where he would sometimes play as a kid. His family was a typical middle-class American family. He went to college and was a jewelry designer by trade, but he also worked as a banker in downtown Seattle for two years. When we got married, he told everyone he wanted only two children because he wanted to keep things manageable. (If you read chapter 9, you know how that story turned out!)

My growing-up years looked a little different. My family moved around a lot, but I grew up mainly in the farm country of the Central Valley in California, which was surrounded by vineyards, cotton fields, and almond trees. I have fond memories of walking home from our little country school down dusty dirt roads, stopping along the way to feel the cool water gushing out of the irrigation pipes and flowing down the long rows of cotton fields. I lived in the suburbs of some Southern California cities as well, so I had a little more experience with different living situations than my husband. My time living in the country was by far my favorite.

Seizing Your Opportunities

As Darryl and I began to have kids, we decided that, if possible, we would like to raise them out in the country. We wanted to give them a homespun childhood. The thought of our kids being able to run free and spend lots of time outdoors resonated with our hearts. We also thought it would be great to have a few animals. We realized, however, that neither of us actually enjoyed caring for animals. We decided to wait and see if our kids really wanted them, and then to wait until they were old enough to provide most of the care the animals needed.

As I mentioned previously, our oldest daughter, Brittney, turned out to be an animal lover, so before we knew it, we had cats, dogs, chickens, horses, ponies, sheep, milking goats, and a llama. We even had a milk cow two different times. Brittney loved them all and took meticulous care of them. Of course, her younger siblings participated in the responsibilities, and we shared countless lessons together over the years as we dealt with birth, death, sickness, baby animals born with disabilities, animals escaping their pens, feeding and milking schedules, predators, inclement weather, and more.

Many people would call our country life ideal for homeschooling, maybe even perfect. I can assure you, however, that it was not perfect. While I would agree that our circumstances had certain advantages, I would also say that the biggest advantages had nothing to do with creating the perfect homeschooling scenario. It was more about recognizing the opportunities in front of us. God fulfilled our desire to live in the country by providing a home on some acreage when our oldest was twelve. She had a strong desire to have animals, and our other kids wanted them as well.

There were days when I wondered why in the world we were doing this. It was a lot of work to keep on hand all the supplies necessary to take good care of the animals. We also had to check that our kids were doing their part of the chores. It took time, money, and occasionally even our health. Although Darryl is highly allergic to hay, he fought off sneezing attacks and labored breathing in order to move several tons of hay with our boys every fall so that the animals would have what they needed over the harsh winter months.

Every time I stopped and asked God if we could please do something else (preferably something easier), he reminded me of the opportunities in front of us. He showed me how much our kids were thriving and learning and assured me he was using it to prepare them for what he had in store.

Our kids often share how our life together helped them develop problem-solving skills (critical thinking), a work ethic, responsibility, and so much more. God used their experiences to build within them a framework of principles. These principles are what have shaped who they are and how they view life. A few of our children have chosen a similar life as they have begun to have their own kids, but the framework is present in all the kids, no matter where and how they have chosen to live. They know they can draw from the principles they learned while they were growing up and apply them to many scenarios.

You don't need to move your kids to the country or raise farm animals to instill good life principles. You simply need to recognize the opportunities God has for you and your kids. He will use those opportunities to prepare your kids for what he has in store.

As Christians who live in an affluent culture, we tend to become discontented easily. We have more choices than many generations before us, which is a blessing, but it can also be a curse when our choices distract us from embracing the life God has given us. We can become consumed with trying to create what we believe is the perfect scenario instead of standing firmly on one of the most powerful biblical truths: the sovereignty of God.

Here's a principle I learned early on that not only shaped my perspective on life, but also on the way I raised and homeschooled our kids: "Look for where God is working and join him in his work." It was so simple, yet so profound.

I have often made the mistake of thinking I always have to be the initiator, working *hard* to *make* things happen, forgetting that God is already at work. When I start feeling stressed or overwhelmed, it's important to pause and ask for discernment and wisdom to know how to best navigate putting my kids' needs over the schedule, if need be. I may have my own agenda, but my plans will always pale in comparison to his plans.

I can rest in the fact that God is almighty, sovereign, good, and always working. I can trust that his plan is so much better, and I can simply join in the work he is already doing when I see it. His work is perfect in all ways, perfectly weaving together both timing and circumstances.

What does this look like in reality? I have often had plans for my day that I was excited about and assumed were also God's plans, only to have them derailed by a cranky baby, a needy toddler, or a teen who needed to talk. But God clearly calls us to put relationships and people first. I learned from those situations that I was sometimes so invested in what I thought was God's plan for the day that I found myself resistant to the possibility that God may have had something different for me in that moment.

Faith is acting on what God has revealed about his will and character. We know from Scripture that God calls us to pay attention to those who are in need (James 2:15–16; Proverbs 3:27). He also tells us that parents are to prioritize caring for their families (1 Timothy 5:8). So when I have needy children, I can safely assume this is where God is working in the moment, and I need to join in what he is already doing.

As I love that cranky baby or comfort the needy toddler, as I spend time listening to my teen and encouraging him to share his heart with me, I am joining in the work that God is already doing in the lives of my kids. Raising families is a valuable and God-ordained mission. It's a ministry, and like all ministries, it involves meeting needs.

There will also be times that we can't immediately meet a need, and it's important to be tuned into that as well. Sometimes, the work God is doing is teaching our kids a little bit of patience by having to wait their turn or directing us to engage other children to help.

When we homeschool, it's easy to become consumed with making sure our kids have everything they need in every moment. Our intentions may be good and come from a place of not wanting to fail our kids, but we can be treading on dangerous territory here. Without meaning to, we may send the message that the world revolves around them.

No parent wants to raise selfish kids, but raising kids who are others-oriented happens only when we help our kids realize they are not the center of the universe. In other words, it's OK if there are times your children need to wait to have their needs met because you have something you need to accomplish.

This is why I always encourage parents not to give up their own hobbies or interests when they choose to homeschool. We sometimes have to make sacrifices in order to homeschool our kids, but we shouldn't be too quick to part with the things we love, because those things can teach our kids life lessons as well.

Health and nutrition have always been interests of mine, so I love taking recipes and trying to make them healthier. I also enjoy finding alternative, natural ways to help our family get over illnesses and injuries, so I read, research, and experiment a lot simply because I enjoy it. My husband and I took an herb class together and learned to recognize herbs in the wild and how to use them for healing, tinctures, poultices, and teas. I was often so excited about what I was learning or making that I talked to our kids about it and invited them to work alongside me.

This may not have been an area of interest for all of them, but my enthusiasm often naturally drew them into what I was doing. The benefit to them wasn't dependent on whether or not they were keenly interested in the same topics as I was, but rather that they saw an example of what it looks like to be a lifelong learner. I was excited about learning, I was being resourceful, and I pursued my interests. I was a living example of our family's mission: growing life-long learners, being resourceful, and having a strong work ethic. The kids didn't have to love what I was doing, but they could choose to be excited about it with and for me. Whether or not they did was up to them, and they learned in the process that everything doesn't revolve around them.

I also had priorities related to our family life that included everything from preparing simple and healthy meals to maintaining a consistent routine with regular mealtimes, naps, and bedtimes. I needed those things, and my kids needed them. Because these priorities were important to me, they were part of what revealed my reality. Any schoolwork that involved books or curriculum had to revolve around these priorities. It was how our family functioned best in that season.

What that ended up looking like in the early years was that I could only seem to pull off three mornings a week of bookwork with my school-age kids. I tried and tried for more, but it was an exercise in futility. Finally, I prayed about it and felt peace. If this was our reality, I could trust God with it. He was sovereign over our family, and each of our kids arrived on the scene when he wanted them to. He knew what he was doing, and I had to trust him. To paraphrase Keith Green, I just kept doing my best and prayed it would be blessed, and that Jesus would take care of the rest. And he did.

Twenty-something years later, I can see clearly that my kids are no worse off for living our reality in that season. In fact, I think they are better off. We were immersed in real life together. They were learning to engage toddlers in meaningful play, change diapers, identify needs and meet them, follow directions, clean up after themselves and others, prepare simple and nutritious food, bond with their siblings, and much more. Their skills quickly grew along with their confidence.

When our kids know they are an important part of a bigger picture, and the people they love are depending on them even in the simplest ways, they know they have value. Why is that? Because God created us to be productive and to love and serve one another. At our house, school revolved around family life, not family life around school. Education was a priority, but education wasn't limited to reading, writing, and math. It was about learning how to live and love well. The goal was to live a balanced life with biblical priorities as our foundation.

I strongly encourage you to spend some time prayerfully taking stock of your family's reality—your real needs and circumstances—during this season. What breathes life into your family? What brings peace? What is simply not working for you, and what things are non-negotiable? What do you need to prioritize?

As this becomes clearer, the life God intends for your family will gently unfold. Trust in his goodness, and ask him to give you the eyes to see how he might use your current season and circumstances to shape and prepare your kids for life.

This isn't a one-and-done kind of practice. You will need to revisit these questions and make adjustments to your routine along the way because circumstances change, our kids change, and we change. The good news is that God does not change. He is faithful and will gently lead you through every season, allowing you to walk in freedom and truly enjoy these years with your kids.

1. Do you believe God is working all the time? Do you believe he has a good plan and wisdom for the life you are living today?

2. Make a list of opportunities (educational or otherwise) that you have right where you live. What might be the best way to take advantage of these? Ask God for wisdom!

3. Spend part of a day watching and documenting where you see God working.

4. What priorities do you want to live out in your current season?

CHAPTER 15

Community Is Crucial

Finding Your Tribe

As I looked around at many of my homeschooling friends, I began to wonder if there was something wrong with me. For example, my friend Heidi seemed to be able to pull off homeschooling as well as involvement in women's ministry and our church worship team. To top it all off, she saw a need at our church for a homeschool co-op and decided to start one herself.

I, on the other hand, felt a great sense of accomplishment if I could get the grocery shopping done and keep everyone fed, clothed, bathed, and rested while simultaneously keeping the house from falling apart around me. In order for our family to function well, we had to keep a simple routine and stay home much of the time.

Our oldest was nine, and we had just had our sixth baby. When Heidi asked if I wanted to be part of the co-op, I felt like the least I could do was give it a try. Besides, it sounded like a great fit. Our kids would have the opportunity to take some classes, maybe learn things I couldn't teach them, and have fun with their friends.

What I didn't anticipate was how incredibly hard it would be to get six kids out the door on Friday mornings. It didn't help that the three oldest kids were the only ones old enough to attend classes, while the youngest three needed to be in the nursery. The youngest two were still in diapers, and our three-month-old was still nursing every three hours.

A parent-led co-op only works if the parents are involved, so I needed to either teach a class or help in a class during the time we were attending. Needless to say, it felt like too much. A few weeks into the semester, I waved the white flag and decided that home was the best place for us in that season. I felt relieved.

Heidi was understanding, assuring me that I had to do what was best for our family. If that meant not participating in the co-op, then I should do it. That lesson stuck with me for a long time. It helped me to be more content in living out our family's reality in that season. As a result, we were able to find a daily rhythm that gave us the peace we knew God wanted for us.

A few years later, we moved across the state to a more rural setting. We were living on ten acres and planned to continue our simple life at home. We didn't know anyone in the community at first, but then started attending a small church and were thrilled to find that most of the families were homeschoolers. We began getting to know them and kept hearing about a parent partnership program in which many of the families were involved. We were hesitant at first because we were still adjusting to living in a new place. I wanted to be sure we had found a rhythm for our family before we added anything new to our daily routine.

Eventually, we became convinced that we should at least check out the program. By that time, we had seven kids, and four of them were old enough to attend classes. I was not required to be there to teach or bring our littles for that one day a week. I could hang out in the moms' room with the little ones or go home if I wanted, and our older kids could attend for half a day or all day. We had options.

I spent a lot of time in the moms' room because I wanted to be sure this place was a good fit for my kids and to be available if they needed me. I also wanted to get to know the other families in order to find out more about the people my kids were spending time with. It didn't take long before I discovered that these were my people. They had chosen a homeschooling lifestyle for many of the same reasons we had, and though they chose to walk it out in different ways, many of us lived similar lives. Most of us lived on several acres, raised animals, and planted gardens. Despite the fact that it was a public school program, most of the families shared a common faith. It was the framework within which we were all living, and it was foundational to our parenting, how we treated people, and how we approached life.

The woman who ran the program had homeschooled all six of her children, now grown. Most of the teachers were parents of the kids who attended the program. It was well organized and didn't feel anything like a public school. It was more like being on a homeschool island while still enjoying some of the benefits of the traditional school setting. But more than anything, it was about finding community.

Our kids loved the program, and it served our family well for twelve years. I will be forever grateful for the opportunities our kids had there. God used that experience to enrich our home education. It also gifted us with friendships, many of which continue to this day.

Support Is Essential

Homeschooling can be a lonely journey, especially in contexts where home education is a divisive topic. Many families experience hostility from friends and family when they decide to homeschool. I've heard some horrible stories, which breaks my heart, because the decision to homeschool is not typically a random or impulsive one.

What kind of parent just casually decides to homeschool, which means being with their kids 24/7? It's not a parent who is trying to shirk their responsibilities, that's for sure. It's a parent who has thought long and hard about what they believe is best for their kids and has decided they are willing to face the challenge head-on for the sake of their children. This is why homeschooling parents are often fiercely protective of each other. We have all dealt with some amount of resistance as a result of our decision, and we feel an obligation to provide support to others who are struggling. Because we tend to be small in number, we have had to stick together, and we do that best when we are in community with one another.

Even the most introverted person needs support, which is why God created us for community. The wise writer of Ecclesiastes put it this way:

> Two people are better off than one, for they can help each other succeed. If one person falls, the other can reach out and help. But someone who falls alone is in real trouble. Likewise, two people lying close together can keep each other warm. But how can one be warm alone? A person standing alone can be attacked and defeated, but two can stand back-to-back and conquer. Three are even better, for a triple-braided cord is not easily broken. (Eccl. 4:9–12)

I love what a clear and hopeful picture this passage gives us. It can help us recognize when we have found our tribe. Can you see yourself standing back-to-back with the people you would call your tribe?

If you are new to homeschooling, the thought of finding your tribe might feel intimidating or perhaps even scary. Many people make assumptions about homeschoolers, one of which is that we all do things the same way. Nothing could be farther from the truth! It's true that twenty-five to thirty years ago, we may have looked more similar, but the homeschooling community has grown exponentially since then and is now a very diverse group.

On the upside, this means our options for community are vaster and more varied; on the downside, because communities can be more specialized, it may take longer to find a group in which you feel at home. Until we find our tribe, we might have a season of loneliness.

Once again, it's important to remember that God is sovereign. Continue to pray for the right community. Simply having another family to get together with works the best in some seasons. Pray with your kids. Watch for how God might be using this season of loneliness to reveal himself to you and your family, and then pray some more! He is faithful.

As you are praying and waiting, here are four things to keep in mind that will help you decide whether or not a community or tribe is a good fit for you.

Know Your Priorities

I struggled when I had to make a decision to forego attending that first co-op, because it seemed like a great fit. But it came down to doing what was best for our family in that season. It's important to know your priorities as a family and to keep these in mind when looking for your tribe.

Here are some questions to consider.

What daily routine and lifestyle fits your family best? If your kids love being outside, maybe a group that plans a lot of outdoor activities would be a good fit.

What season of life are you in? If you have younger children, home is often the best place to be most of the time in order to meet their ongoing needs like naps and regular feeding times. Considering the needs of our family as a whole helps us make better decisions.

How often are you willing to leave the house? Some groups require a lot of on-site participation, which may or may not work well for you.

What days work best for you to be away from home? It's important to keep a good rhythm at home. Our kids need a certain amount of consistency. It provides much-needed security. I always say that life should be a series of adventures launched from a secure home base. Keep that home base solid.

What are you hoping to find in a homeschool group? Are you looking for other moms to connect with so you don't feel alone, enrichment for your children's interests, tutoring in specific areas, a chance for your kids to be outside more?

Are you looking for socialization? Remember, socialization can happen anywhere. It doesn't have to be in a school-like group setting, especially during the early years. However, from about junior high age on, it can be very beneficial. Just be open to thinking outside the box. For instance, older kids can socialize while planning an event, volunteering with a group of other kids, attending a youth group gathering, or getting a group of kids together for a night of games and popcorn. It can be fun and educational for them to come up with ideas, do the planning, and be responsible for the event. It doesn't have to be formal; it can be spontaneous. Do whatever works best for you and your kids.

What kind of kids do you want your kids to spend time with? We aren't trying to cloister our kids in a perfect environment, but as parents, we have the right and the responsibility to discern what kind of people we're considering as our community, and what our kids might be exposed to through those people. This is a personal decision because, ultimately, parents are accountable for these decisions.

Do you want your kids to experience having to meet someone else's requirements in a classroom setting? I found it helpful for my kids to have to meet another teacher's expectations, especially starting in junior high and high school.

Is the setting a good fit for your child? If your child is a hands-on learner, don't expect a class that centers around a textbook to be beneficial. But if you believe your child is ready for that experience, or they really want to participate, it might be a good fit.

We don't want to commit to something only to have it throw off the rhythm we've worked so hard to establish for our family. Being true to our priorities will help keep that from happening.

Know Your Kids

I always encourage parents to continually be a student of their kids. What are their interests? What piques their curiosity? What makes their faces light up? When do you see learning happening?

When you're considering joining a co-op, another important question is, do your kids *want* to be part of a co-op? Sometimes the decision is as simple as that. I might have lofty hopes about all the ways I believe my child would benefit from a co-op, but if my child really doesn't want to go, it might not be the right time yet.

Don't Try to Force Something That Is Not Meant to Be

Whether it's a friendship with another family or becoming involved in a homeschool group, it's important to be willing to let it go, if necessary. Forced situations of any kind only bring more stress into our lives. The difficulties and resistance we experience when forcing something could also be God's way of saying that it's not a good fit for us.

Some things are simply seasonal, even friendships. They work well in one season but not another. God is gracious and has ways of revealing that to us. One of those ways is when things start to feel forced. Again, it comes back to living your reality. The homeschooling journey is different for each family. Sometimes our paths intersect with the paths of others for a while and then separate, going in different directions. At other times, God just has us in a season of waiting.

Whenever you find yourself in a lonely season, it's a good time to have conversations with our kids about where we are putting our trust. Are we going to pray and trust God to bring what we need when we need it? It's an opportunity to model to our kids that God is faithful.

Trust That God Is Enough

Even as adults, this can be a challenging principle to embrace and walk out, but as we do, our kids will see that we serve a very real God who has good things for us even when our circumstances feel hard. When our actions and attitudes communicate our belief that God is enough, we prepare our kids for real life by modeling a deep trust in God's sovereignty and goodness. We show them what it looks like that "godliness with contentment is great gain" (1 Tim. 6:6–8 NIV). Contentment isn't natural; it's intentional. Intentionally walking out our faith day by day in the here and now will impact our kids more deeply than any Sunday school lesson or Bible curriculum.

When I look back over our homeschooling years, the people who have been the richest part of our lives and who stood back-to-back with us have been those whose faith was essential to every part of their lives. These were the people who were determined to stick together through the most difficult parts of our journey and theirs. They rejoiced when we rejoiced and mourned when we mourned, and we did the same for them.

No tribe or community is perfect, but community is part of God's design. God is a community in himself: Father, Son, and Holy Spirit. We were created to bear his image, so it makes sense that we need each other. Our culture often encourages autonomy, but the truth is that God gave us each other to walk alongside, encourage, and spur one another on (Heb. 10:24, 25).

Finally, life can throw some pretty big curveballs, and in some seasons, gathering with a group on a regular basis is simply not realistic. There were several years when my main lifeline was one friend on whom I leaned when the days were hard, mundane, or worth celebrating. My friend

Jana was that person to me. She had seven kids, so she understood the chaos that could erupt in a nanosecond, but she also shared my passion for raising a godly family. We encouraged each other with everything from biblical reminders to hysterical laughter. We leaned into each other for prayer and got together in person when we could. Like any relationship, there is work involved in building community and friendships, but the benefits can be an immense blessing to our homeschooling journey, enriching it in ways we never imagined.

REAL-LIFE APPLICATION

1. When in your life have you experienced true community? What made that experience meaningful to you and/or your child?

2. When it comes to finding community (or assessing your current community), use the list on pages 182–183 to help give you more clear direction.

3. Make a list of things you know about your child (how they learn best, what piques their curiosity, their ongoing interests, whether they are introverts or extroverts).

4. Is there a chance you may be trying to force something that's not meant to be? (No community or friendship is perfect. It's essential to periodically and prayerfully assess whether they are a good fit in this season of life.)

CHAPTER 16

The Finality of Faith

*Why Passing On Our Faith
to Our Kids Matters*

The kids were laughing hysterically, practically falling out of their chairs, and I couldn't get them to stop.

"Nimrod!" yelled one.

"Pee-leg!" shouted another. This was followed by everyone erupting in laughter again. It was mayhem.

This wasn't what I had pictured when I envisioned reading the Bible to my kids. I thought they would sit and listen with bated breath. I thought they would respectfully refrain from even snickering, appreciating the fact that these were the very words of God.

But here I was, just trying to get through the list of descendants in Genesis so we could move on to the next story, and it didn't appear that we were going to make it past chapter 10, at least not that night.

We found that reading the Bible after dinner, while everyone was still at the table, seemed to work best for us.

We ate dinner together every night at the same time, so it was fairly easy to keep everyone there a little longer for Bible reading and prayer. I'd like to say we were faithfully consistent in remembering to do this nightly through all those years, but the truth is, it was a battle. We would do well for a while, and then suddenly realize it had been several days or a week (or longer) since we had read together.

The funny thing is, if you talk to our grown kids, they will tell you we read the Bible after dinner every single night. In their minds, we were consistent. It's a relief to hear that, especially given the load of guilt I often carried after realizing we had fallen off the wagon *again*. Evidently, the important thing was that we kept getting back on the wagon. God is so gracious and faithful. He saw our hearts, took our imperfect offerings, and multiplied them.

There were times during family devotions when I would have sworn not one of the kids was actually listening. It often seemed as though the lights were on, but no one was home. The boys squirmed and played with their utensils. Every now and then, a fight would randomly break out in the middle of our reading or prayer.

I remember yelling, with frustration in my voice, "Everyone, be quiet! We're trying to pray!" No sooner were the words out of my mouth than I realized what a hypocrite I was, and I had to repent to my kids and God.

I can be pretty determined, but there were times I was just plain whipped and wondered if my persistence was worth it. There was rarely any gratification in the moment when it came to family devotions, but as a believing parent, I knew God had called Darryl and me to pass our faith on to our kids. We both felt strongly that it was the most important gift we could give them. It was also the number one reason we decided to homeschool.

This Old Testament passage was foundational to our decision:

> So commit yourselves wholeheartedly to these words of mine. Tie them to your hands and wear them on your forehead as reminders. Teach them to your children. Talk about them when you are at home and when you are on the road, when you are going to bed and when you are getting up. (Deut. 11:18–19)

When I read this passage, the impression I get is one of discipleship. It's sharing life together, day in and day out, and sharing God with our kids all along the way.

Discipling our kids wasn't optional; it was absolutely crucial, because this wasn't just about our kids—it was also about our grandkids and our great-grandkids. We were making a long-term investment in future generations by investing our faith into the kids God had given us to raise.

The Most Important Thing

Until fifty to sixty years ago, it was common for people in general to have a multi-generational perspective. People lived and made decisions based not solely on what they wanted, but on what would benefit future generations. It inspired those Pilgrim parents to sail on the *Mayflower* in hopes of finding a place where they and their descendants could worship freely. It gave courage to young men who went off to war to defend liberty so that their children and grandchildren would be free. They considered it an honor to give their lives for the next generation. We have been the blessed recipients of their faith and their sacrifice.

This perspective didn't come out of the blue or by

chance; it's rooted in biblical principles. Consider these words spoken by Moses to the people of Israel as they were about to enter the Promised Land after forty years of wandering in the desert:

> Be careful never to forget what you yourself have seen. Do not let these memories escape from your mind as long as you live! And be sure to pass them on to your children and grandchildren. Never forget the day when you stood before the LORD your God at Mount Sinai, where he told me, "Summon the people before me, and I will personally instruct them. Then they will learn to fear me as long as they live, and they will teach their children to fear me also." (Deut. 4:9–10)

In this long-awaited and defining moment, what did God want his people to remember to do from that day forward? He not only wanted them to remember all he had done for them, he wanted them to pass those stories on to their children so that their children would fear (reverence) him as well. Their choices affected generations to come.

In his letter to the church at Ephesus, the apostle Paul wrote that we must raise our children "with the discipline and instruction that comes from the Lord" (Eph. 6:4). The wise writer of Proverbs tells us, "The fear of the LORD is the beginning of wisdom" (Prov. 9:10 NIV). In other words, *all* knowledge and wisdom originate with God, so it's absolutely essential that we pass the fear of the Lord (our faith) on to our kids. Again, it's not optional; it's the very foundation from which they will live their lives.

This is why it didn't matter so much to Darryl and me what our kids decided to do for a living as long as they had an active and personal relationship with God. We wanted them to learn to hear from God for themselves, to recognize his voice, and to walk out what he was directing them to do. In order for them to recognize his voice, they had to know who he is, and Darryl and I had to model biblical principles in our own lives and spend time with other people who did the same.

Jesus used a great illustration that succinctly describes the need for discipleship:

Can one blind person lead another? Won't they both fall into a ditch? Students are not greater than their teacher. But the student who is fully trained will become like the teacher. (Luke 6:39–40)

I see two things here for us as parents.

Children are not born with wisdom. Wisdom has to be learned. Essentially, we could call children foolish (blind to wisdom). Now, picture the traditional classroom setting full of 25–30 kids. As wonderful as a teacher might be, it's not likely that the impact of the teacher's wisdom will outweigh the impact of the foolishness all those children bring to that environment.

Children become like their teacher. When we leave our children with a teacher, how well do we really know that person? Do we know them well enough that we are confident we would like our child to be like them? Even if we are confident, are we willing to let the other children in the class disciple our children? I can guarantee you that is also happening. As parents, the responsibility for who we allow to influence our children falls squarely on our shoulders. When we drop them off at school (or any other place), we are still ultimately responsible before God for the influence teachers and other students have on our children. We are giving them permission to impact our kids for several hours a day, five days a week.

Make no mistake. Education is never neutral. Education is discipleship.

The public school system is a government school system. It is ultimately ruled and funded by the government. In the New Testament, Jesus referred to the government as Caesar (see Matt. 22:21). Pastor and theologian Voddie Baucham wrote, "We cannot continue to send our children to Caesar for their education and be surprised when they come home as Romans."[1] This is exactly what is happening.

According to a recent LifeWay Research report, 66 percent of teens who regularly attended church stop attending when they become young adults.[2] I realize there can be more than one reason for this, but I am also convinced that secular education plays a big part. Again, this is because education is not neutral; when our kids spend that many hours at school, it will greatly impact who they become.

We have the opportunity of a lifetime to influence our children for the kingdom of God. By doing so, we are investing not only into the next generation, but also in the generations that come after that as well. One of the most effective ways we can impact the culture is to raise children who know what it means to "Love the Lord your God with all your heart and with all your soul and with all your strength and with all your mind" and "Love your neighbor as yourself" (Luke 10:27 NIV).

Mother Teresa is credited with saying, "If you want to

change the world, go home and love your family." This doesn't mean we shouldn't minister to people outside our families. It is simply a reminder that our work at home with our kids matters. It is just as much a mission field as any other.

The great thing is that we typically get to disciple our kids from day one. Ask any missionary, and they will tell you that's a luxury they don't have. They generally begin discipleship after a person has experienced much hurt, pain, and brokenness.

From the time our kids are very young, we have the opportunity to expose them to the beauty and goodness of God through nature, music, meaningful conversation, good books, fulfilling experiences, and rich relationships. The impact this has on our children is even more powerful when offered by warm, loving, engaged parents.

A child who grows up in a healthy, godly environment will naturally and willingly learn the things they need to know for successful adulthood with far less stress and a whole lot more joy.

But this lifestyle takes time. It requires us to slow down. We need to listen for God's voice so we can hear his heart for us and for our kids, and so we can focus on discipleship.

Education is discipleship.

Discipleship is rooted in relationships.

Relationships take time.

Let's consider again the words of Jesus: "Students are not greater than their teacher. But the student who is fully trained will become like the teacher" (Luke 6:40). Jesus is saying our kids will become like us—for good *and* for ill. So when we find ourselves acting in a way we wouldn't want them to act, our love for our kids and the call to disciple them can motivate us to humble ourselves, repent of our wrongdoing, and make a change.

This is what a gospel-centered home looks like. It's what gives us hope. None of us are perfect parents or teachers or kids, but that's the point. We don't have to be. Jesus lived the perfect life we couldn't. He died to pay the debt for our sins and then rose again, conquering sin and death *for us*. He bought our freedom, and because of him, there is redemption. He redeems the messy. He turns ashes into beauty. He heals the brokenhearted, and he makes all things beautiful in his time. In other words, it's a process and a journey, but one in which he walks right beside us. He never leaves us nor forsakes us. His mercies are new every morning.

More is caught than taught. Our kids are watching us. As we cling to God's promises and walk in humble obedience to him, we are showing our kids that the God we serve is a powerful, loving, faithful, merciful, just, and good God. As we model this day in and day out, God becomes very real and tangible to our kids, not just a storybook character.

If you are new to the Christian faith, haven't been authentically walking it out, or simply aren't familiar with God's Word, let today be the day that changes that. For the sake of your children and grandchildren, get to know God and his Word and determine to learn right alongside your kids. You'll be astounded at what God does as you walk this journey together. Remember, you are making the investment of a lifetime. Years from now, when you see your grandchildren and great-grandchildren loving and serving him with all their hearts, you will thank God you did!

1. Why does passing on your faith to your child matter? Do you believe faith should be comprehensive? In other words, should it affect every area of life?

2. Do you believe being in God's Word with your child is worth fighting for?

3. Does your child see that your relationship with God is a priority, not in words only but in actions?

4. Do you have a multi-generational perspective?

5. What is your hope and prayer for your child's faith?

6. If you are not familiar with God's Word or are new to the faith, will you purpose to make yourself a student of the Scriptures and bring your children alongside you to learn as well? Be sure to explain to your children why you are making this change, why it's so important, etc.

CHAPTER 17

The Challenge

What Is There to Lose?

Once upon a time, when all of our kids were still at home, I often told them I could never be a foster parent. I greatly respected and admired people who were, but I did not feel called to it. Fast forward. We had just graduated our seventh child and officially had only one left at home. Then, God presented an opportunity for us to provide a home and a family for a young man we barely knew. It wasn't a hard decision. We knew what God's Word says about situations like this: true Christianity is "caring for orphans and widows in their distress" (James 1:27). Almost like a reminder at the perfect time, we felt prompted to read the first two chapters of James just a few days before this opportunity landed in our laps. We took some time to pray, but in the end, the decision felt like a no-brainer.

After we agreed to take the young man into our home, we continued to see the many ways God had prepared us—and prepared Wesley. His presence caused us to pause and think about things we hadn't in a while, and he made us laugh.

At the same time, I am once again at a place I've been countless times over my parenting and homeschooling journey: feeling like I don't have much of a clue what I'm doing or how to walk out the current season well. I have no training, no background in welcoming a new child into the family at seventeen years old. What if we don't understand Wesley, and we somehow make things worse and not better for him? What if the love we try to show him isn't interpreted as love? What if we accidentally communicate more hurt to his already hurting heart? So many questions like these make what we are doing feel risky.

Risk is an action that exposes you to the possibility of loss or injury, but the truth is that genuine love is risky. It makes you vulnerable because you are investing without knowing what the outcome will be.

Look Past the Doubts

We took a risk many years ago when I felt God's nudge to take a more unhurried approach with our kids, focusing on simplicity and relationships. I had no idea how it was all going to turn out. Would I ruin our kids? Would they be ready for the purposes God had for them? Would they resent the fact that we homeschooled them? Would they feel inferior to their peers who had attended public school? Would they be prepared for the "real world"?

What gave me the ability to look past the doubts was the underlying peace I could find only by choosing to walk down that particular path. Nothing else felt right to me. Every other option felt stressful, and I knew a stressed-out mom was the last thing our kids needed. As they looked back on their childhoods, I wanted them to have great memories of a childhood well lived. I wanted them to remember enjoying the innocence, beauty, and simple goodness every child deserves. When they found themselves stressed out as adults, I wanted them to be able to close their eyes, go back to their childhood, and find a happy place that gave them comfort and a sense of calm. These were gifts no one else could give them. It was up to Darryl and me to be the fierce defenders of our kids' childhood. We would have to take the risk, trusting God for the outcome. We had to walk by faith.

Did that mean we never doubted our decisions again? Absolutely not! It meant we had to go back to God again and again for reassurance that we were still on the right track, because there were very often two big enemies knocking on our door—comparisons and distractions.

Comparisons

Let's be honest: there's not a parent out there who hasn't struggled with comparisons. We want our kids to measure up, for their sake and ours. The problem is, we quickly forget that each child is uniquely created with a unique purpose, and that purpose will not be the same for them as it is for anyone else. It's like comparing an apple to an orange. They are both fruits, but they are also entirely different from one another.

When we compare, we do our kids and ourselves a great disservice because, instead of focusing on strengths, we tend to focus on weaknesses. That often causes us to operate from a place of fear, and that never ends well.

I recently came across this acronym for fear:

False
Evidence
Appearing
Real

It's helpful and important to admire strengths in others. However, we're entering the danger zone when comparisons lead us to believe that the progress others are making or the gifts they possess are somehow more valuable than the progress and gifts of our own kids. That's when we're living our lives based on false evidence.

So when I see another child mastering something that is a struggle for my child, I can easily become overfocused on that particular weakness and completely miss the progress my child *is* making, the areas he *is* mastering, and the ways he is using his unique gifts. Suddenly, I feel pressure to push my child by scheduling another class, adding another activity, or buying more curriculum, rather than walking in rhythm with what God has for us and trusting that it is enough for today. The key is recognizing whether or not I am allowing distractions (the second enemy) to draw me away from what is actually a good fit for me and my child. Comparing my child to another is more distracting than helpful. And continually doubting ourselves, worrying that whatever we are doing isn't enough, can quickly take us off course.

Distractions

Distractions are the enemy of direction. When we have a clear vision of where we are going, we are far more intentional. When we are intentional, we are more efficient and effective.

When our kids are allowed to learn through their interests, learning happens much more naturally. Our kids will usually have no idea how much they are learning. When they are firing on all cylinders, multiple things can be learned and absorbed at the same time. It is often so efficient and free of stress that we can very well miss it completely.

When our kids were all younger, they usually spent time

outside in the afternoons. We knew it was good for their health and well-being, and it provided time for me to do some things alone. There were outcroppings of rocks near the house on our property, and the kids would disappear for long periods of time with occasional visits back to the house to use the bathroom or grab "supplies." They were busy and seemed to be having fun. I heard some stories around the dinner table about what they were up to, but it wasn't until years later that I found out just how much they were learning.

Evidently, they created an entire "civilization" amongst those rock outcroppings. They each had their own property with boundary lines and dwellings they constructed from old sheets or cardboard, scrap wood, metal roofing, whatever they could find, certain rules they all agreed to live by, and their own currency. They bartered, bought and sold goods, made agreements, and learned to negotiate. Each of them played a different role in their society: some were doctors, others were law enforcement or farmers, and two of the youngest ones were store owners. Why? Because they were the most likely to be able to talk Mom into giving them snacks they could then turn around and "sell" in their civilization.

Our adult kids have told me that there were so many things they learned through role-playing in that civilization that they have applied to real life. At the time, allowing them to spend afternoons outside felt like taking a risk; I had to trust that outside play was constructive and would be enough for that season of our lives. Instead of panicking and thinking I had to *make* learning happen, I allowed our family to create its own rhythm by doing what came naturally, what brought peace, what encouraged sibling relationships, and what worked for me as a mom at the time.

Fortunately, the results were that learning did become efficient and effective, but it first required me to let go of preconceived ideas about what education looked like. I had to be willing to open my heart and hands to something new, trusting that it would be so much better for our kids. It meant I had to take a risk.

Big Returns

Darryl has always said that the riskiest investments have the greatest potential for big returns. Our kids are not only a lifetime investment; they are an eternal investment. We have to ask ourselves what we are willing to risk for the sake of our kids.

Are we willing to risk the disapproval of others or the fact that our child may never look like someone else's? Are we willing to risk that our kids' education may look a bit odd to others even though it feels just right for us? Will we risk that our kids may not test well, even though we know they are learning to use their gifts in amazing ways? Will we risk making faith a central focus for our family, trusting that God will show us the nuts and bolts our kids need along the way?

Consider the risks of the alternatives and options you have in front of you. Are you ready for a much-needed change? Are you more convinced than ever that when it comes to education, there is a better way? Are you ready to experience a bold adventure that will change the course of your family for the good?

In the words of Ms. Frizzle from *The Magic School Bus*, "Take chances, make mistakes, get messy!" The difference between success and failure doesn't lie in how smart we are or how many resources we have. It's about being willing to learn.

Parents, I'm challenging you today to give home education a try for one school year. I guarantee you will not destroy your child's education in that amount of time. Are you willing to take a risk? Taking a risk is not the same as wasting time. No time invested in your child is ever wasted.

More parents than ever are seeing that there is a better way to educate their kids, and it doesn't require spending eight hours a day teaching them. What I've shared in this book is a much more efficient and effective approach and one that allows our families to thrive. It starts with warm, loving, engaged parents who are willing to adventure off the beaten path of a one-size-fits-all education in pursuit of a lifestyle that is not only more conducive to building strong families, but one that will give our kids a rich, full education.

You can do this.

REAL-LIFE APPLICATION

1. Is it possible God may be calling you to look past doubt and fear, take a risk, and trust him in home educating your child?

2. Are you beginning to sense some peace about the possibilities?

3. If you could homeschool your child with all fears and comparisons removed, how would you go about it?

4. In this chapter, I said, "Our kids are not only a lifetime investment; they are an eternal investment. We have to ask ourselves what we are willing to risk for the sake of our kids." What are you willing to risk for the sake of your kids (what others think, their education looking "different," walking by faith)?

5. If you aren't home educating yet, are you willing to accept the challenge to homeschool your child for one year? Why or why not?

Acknowledgments

How do I begin to acknowledge the vast number of people God has sovereignly woven into my life over the last five-plus decades? I could write a completely separate book filled with the names of those who have left a lasting imprint on my life and, consequently, helped write this book.

To my husband, Darryl. I'll never forget those words you whispered to me at the altar on our wedding day all those years ago: "We are going to have a great life!"

I had no idea at the time what that meant or what it would look like, but almost thirty-two years later, I can honestly say you were spot-on. I'd be lying if I said things were always easy, but somehow, in the midst of grief, loss, trials, pain, and the countless challenges that have been part of our journey, we have, in fact, had a great life. I am deeply thankful for every day that I am still living it with you.

Brittney, I can still feel the hot tears running down my face when you were placed in my arms for the first time. You were the culmination of my life dream: to be a mom. Of course, I had no idea at the time that you would be the oldest of an entire tribe, but you have worn the badge of the oldest child with honor. You are still so much of the glue that holds our family together as you continue to be mindful of how your siblings are doing at any given moment, in spite of the fact that you are now a wife and wonderful mom to four little ones.

Jenna, I remember how tiny you were as a baby. The saying, "Though she is little, she is fierce," always seemed like a perfect description of you. You have always thought and felt deeply. Those are not always easy gifts to live with, but you have somehow taken them and used them well. You are not afraid to challenge the status quo. You are fully and beautifully embracing your life as a wife and mom, and I couldn't be prouder.

Jake, I'll forever remember your curly blond locks and big blue eyes looking up at me at three years old as you explained how you figured something out or built something that even MacGyver would be proud of. You were the first of a crew of four boys born in just under six years. You've been a stellar example to your brothers of determination and hard work, but more importantly, of kindness. We are proud of you and your accomplishments, but mostly of the man you've become.

Ben, as a little guy, every morning like clockwork, you would toddle into the kitchen with a smile on your face, (not to mention those dimples) and greet us with a "good goming" (good morning), followed by a hug. Your consistent joy over the years has been an ongoing example to our whole family. You are kind, generous, and hard-working—and if I ever need survival skills, I know exactly who to call!

Luke, from a very young age, you were painfully aware of injustice and were not one to let it slide. You are a truth-seeker and won't settle for anything less, which is both honorable and entertaining at times as you often express what many think but are afraid to say. Your name means "bearer of light," and that is exactly what you are.

Sam, you were determined to keep up with your older brothers, which proved to be challenging in many ways. Ultimately, it inspired maturity in you at an early age. You've worked and wrestled for the important things while maintaining a sense of humor that keeps our family laughing.

Johanna, God knew what he was doing when he placed you in the midst of a bunch of boys. Somehow, you wrapped every one of them around your finger. You've always been the perfect combination of sweet and salty. You love the girly things, but you aren't afraid to get your hands dirty. Your passion for God and his Word is an inspiration to me!

Silas, your entrance into life rocked our world, and you continued to bring surprises all along the way. I don't think I will ever recover from all the times you wandered off in search of some adventure! Now, you are well on your way to manhood, and oh, how I love our conversations as we walk out these last years of homeschooling.

Dad and Mom, my childhood was a gift that I will always treasure. Though you were only teenagers when you became parents, you both decided you would pour your time and energy into the lives of your kids. You saw us as a worthwhile and long-term investment. The message that we were valuable and loved was clearly conveyed. Like every parent, you were learning as you went, but you worked hard to instill in us a deep faith, a solid sense of right and wrong, a strong work ethic, resilience, and the incredible value of family. Our children and grandchildren continue to benefit greatly from your investment. Thank you.

Carolann, you have been a presence in my life since I was eighteen years old. You were there the day Darryl and I were married and have celebrated the births of each of our children as though they were your own grandchildren. You have rejoiced with me; you have mourned with me. You have done it all firmly planted in God's faithfulness and have brought me back to his truths and promises over and over again. In doing so, you have given me what I truly needed: a confidence that he is enough. You continually hold my heart and hand as I walk through each season of life, and I am infinitely richer for it. You are both my mentor and my friend.

Kathie, you have known me for the last twenty-three years, and your encouragement has come in the moments I needed it most. You've set your clock and lost sleep in order to pray for me at the specific times that I needed it. It has meant more than you know. My prayer is that you will get to tell your magnificent God story on the pages of your own book someday.

Mr. Clancy, I am so thankful you were my teacher. Because our school was small, you were the only teacher I had for two years (seventh and eighth grade), and I will be forever grateful. Your love and care for your students was obvious as you balanced encouragement and discipline. You seemed to know what each student needed and invested accordingly. The way you taught and led your students positively impacted our homeschooling in countless ways. Because of this, your influence continues on to my grandchildren.

Teresa, I had no idea when we met over forty years ago that our friendship would be a lifelong one, but I couldn't be more grateful. There are so many things I never have to say or explain to you because you know me so well. Friendships like that are a rare jewel, and I will forever treasure ours.

Ginger, when we were homeschooling all those years ago with the "Wise Words of Wisdom Chart" hanging on our wall, I never imagined that the creator of that little chart would become a dear friend many years later! Our connection was instant, and our friendship is most certainly a blessing from God. When you said, "Durenda, I think you have another book in you," you were absolutely right and have continued to be one of my greatest cheerleaders as I worked on this project! Thank you, friend, from the bottom of my heart!

Sara, having our children grow up alongside each other has a way of bringing two moms together! I always walk away from our conversations better off than when I came. You have a unique ability to clarify thoughts and ideas that help me express with words what's in my heart. To me, that is what a true friend does, and I will always treasure our friendship!

Beth, when I finally embraced my gift of writing, I kept hearing your sweet voice from all those years ago, encouraging me to write. I thought you were just being sweet (which wasn't unusual for you). Eventually, I realized those nudges were actually little seeds sown that God watered and slowly grew over many years. Thank you for being faithful to plant those seeds.

Jana, my children should probably be the ones to thank you since I'm convinced that you saved their lives on several occasions by simply answering your phone and talking me off the ledge. It was a privilege to share that particular season with you. God knew exactly what we both needed!

Pastor Wes, the last two years of sitting under your teaching have challenged me and brought significant growth in my life. Finding a pastor who handles the Word of God with clarity and precision is a rarity these days. Thank you for committing yourself wholeheartedly to the study and understanding of Scripture and equipping your flock well.

Teresa, my literary agent, what an amazing couple of years this has been! You have been such a constant source of encouragement and thoughtfulness as we walked through this process together. I'm incredibly grateful for your experience and the way you poured yourself into this project!

The Zondervan team, it's amazing to me how people

I'd never met until several months ago have become like family. The expertise and care with which everyone on the team handles their roles clearly reveal that this isn't just a job but something they are passionate about. I am grateful to be a recipient of such talent, experience, and resources.

Notes

Chapter 1: Education: A New Frontier

1. Ken Robinson, quoted in Jessica Shepherd, "Fertile Minds Need Feeding," *The Guardian*, February 9, 2009, https://www.theguardian.com/education/2009/feb/10/teaching-sats.

Chapter 3: The Sacred Cow

1. "Sacred cow," Vocabulary.com, https://www.vocabulary.com/dictionary/sacred%20cow.
2. Kevin Mahnken, "Sixty-one Percent of Teachers Stressed Out, 58 Percent Say Mental Health Is Not Good in New National Survey," *The 74*, October 31, 2017, https://www.the74million.org/61-of-teachers-stressed-out-58-say-mental-health-is-not-good-in-new-national-survey/.
3. Margaret Weigel, "No Child Left Behind and Education Outcomes: Research Roundup," The Journalist's Resource: Informing the News, August 25, 2011, https://journalistsresource.org/politics-and-government/nclb-no-child-left-behind-research/.
4. Lauren Camera, "U.S. Students Show No Improvement in Math, Reading, Science on International Exam," *U.S. News & World Report*, December 3, 2019, https://www.usnews.com/news/education-news/articles/2019-12-03/us-students-show-no-improvement-in-math-reading-science-on-international-exam.
5. To read more on this subject, see Mike Margeson and Justin

Spears, "The History and Results of America's Disastrous Public School System, Part I," Foundation for Economic Education, May 13, 2019, https://fee.org/articles/the-history -and-results-of-our-disastrous-public-school-system-part-i/. See also John Taylor Gatto, *Weapons of Mass Instruction: A Schoolteacher's Journey through the Dark World of Compulsory Schooling* (Canada: New Society Publishers, 2010).

Chapter 4: Teaching through Your Child's Passion

1. C. S. Lewis, *Surprised by Joy: The Shape of My Early Life* (New York: HarperCollins, 1955, 2017), 137.
2. John Holt, *How Children Learn*, rev. ed. (New York: Da Capo Press, 2017), xii.
3. John Holt, *Learning All the Time: How Small Children Begin to Read, Write, Count, and Investigate the World, without Being Taught* (New York: Da Capo Press, 1990), 162.
4. Sir Ken Robinson, "Bring On the Learning Revolution!" TED2010, February 2010, https://www.ted.com/talks/sir _ken_robinson_bring_on_the_learning_revolution#t-997123.

Chapter 5: Who's Driving the Bus? Nurturing Independent Learners

1. Chris Churchill, "Churchill: Remembering John Taylor Gatto," *Times Union*, August 10, 2019, https://www.timesunion.com /7dayarchive/article/Churchill-Remembering-John-Taylor -Gatto-14291234.php.
2. John Holt, *Learning All the Time: How Small Children Begin to Read, Write, Count, and Investigate the World, without Being Taught* (New York: Da Capo Press, 1990), 160.

Chapter 6: Educating for Life, Not Just Graduation

1. Tim Elmore, *Marching Off the Map: Inspire Students to Navigate a Brand New World* (Atlanta, GA: Poet Gardener Publishing, 2017), 10–11.
2. Alexandra Twin, "Long-Term Investments," Investopedia,

March 16, 2020, https://www.investopedia.com/terms
/l/longterminvestments.asp.

3. Elmore, *Marching Off the Map*, 74.

4. Kathy Koch, *Five to Thrive: How to Determine If Your Core Needs Are Being Met (and What to Do When They're Not)*, (Chicago: Moody Publishers, 2020), 71.

5. Timothy Keller, *The Meaning of Marriage: Facing the Complexities of Commitment with the Wisdom of God* (New York: Penguin Books, 2011), 101.

Chapter 9: In the Beginning: Babies and Toddlers

1. "Discernment," Wikipedia, https://en.wikipedia.org/wiki/Discernment.

Chapter 10: Nurturing Seedlings: The Early School Years

1. Durenda Wilson, *The Unhurried Homeschooler: A Simple, Mercifully Short Book on Homeschooling* (CreateSpace, 2016), 19.

2. John Holt, *Learning All the Time: How Small Children Begin to Read, Write, Count, and Investigate the World, without Being Taught* (New York: Da Capo Press, 1990), 4.

3. Leigh Eagar, interviewed in *Weirdos: A Homeschool Documentary*, directed by Matt Black, Vimeo, May 23, 2020, https://vimeo.com/ondemand/weirdos.

4. See "Learning through Play," https://en.wikipedia.org/wiki/Learning_through_play, and "Why Young Kids Need Less Class Time—and More Play Time—at School," *Washington Post*, August 21, 2015, https://www.washingtonpost.com/news/answer-sheet/wp/2015/08/21/why-young-kids-need-less-class-time-and-more-play-time-at-school/.

Chapter 11: Growing Confidence: The Middle Years

1. Carol Dweck, quoted in "Growth Mindset," Glossary of Education Reform, August 29, 2013, https://www.edglossary.org/growth-mindset/.

2. One thing that really helps with these conversations and challenges is to understand more about different personalities and love languages, because those greatly affect a person's response. There are plenty of great personality and love language tests you can find online that take only minutes to fill out but will give you a much clearer perspective on both yourself and your child.

3. "How Does Writing Affect Your Brain?" NeuroRelay, August 7, 2013, http://neurorelay.com/2013/08/07/how-does-writing-affect-your-brain/.

4. "What Is a 'Living Book'?" Simply Charlotte Mason, https://simplycharlottemason.com/faq/livingbook/.

5. Sarah Mackenzie, *The Read-Aloud Family: Making Meaningful and Lasting Connections with Your Kids* (Grand Rapids: Zondervan, 2018), 70.

6. Alycia Zimmerman, "Using LEGO to Build Math Concepts," Scholastic, May 19, 2016, https://www.scholastic.com/teachers/blog-posts/alycia-zimmerman/using-lego-build-math-concepts/.

Chapter 12: The Sky's the Limit: The Final School Years

1. Paul David Tripp, *Age of Opportunity: A Biblical Guide to Parenting Teens* (Phillipsburg, NJ: P&R Publishing, 2001), 138–139.

2. At this age, helping kids learn more about self-development is both beneficial and an important path toward becoming a healthy adult. It's the perfect time to walk this out with our kids, as teens typically feel a need to find out more about who they are. In her book, *More Than Credits*, Cheryl Bastian guides parents as they walk alongside their teens and young adults through five personal development credits. She shares resources and alternatives to help teens learn practical skills through personalized, project-based learning.

3. Sandra Aamodt, interviewed by Tony Cox, "Brain Maturity Extends Well Beyond Teen Years," *Tell Me More*, radio

broadcast, October 10, 2011, https://www.npr.org /templates/story/story.php?storyId=141164708.

Chapter 13: The Nature of Things

1. "Jordan Peterson," Wikipedia, https://en.wikipedia.org /wiki/Jordan_Peterson.
2. Michael Gurian and Kathy Stevens, *The Minds of Boys: Saving Our Sons from Falling Behind in School and Life* (San Francisco: Jossey Bass, 2005), 51.

Chapter 16: The Finality of Faith: Why Passing On Our Faith to Our Kids Matters

1. Voddie Baucham Jr., *Family Driven Faith: Doing What It Takes to Raise Sons and Daughters Who Walk with God* rev. ed. (Wheaton, IL: Crossway Books, 2011), loc. 3321 of 4121, Kindle.
2. "Most Teenagers Drop Out of Church as Young Adults," LifeWay Research, January 15, 2019, https://lifewayresearch.com/2019/01/15/most -teenagers-drop-out-of-church-as-young-adults/.